Meeting in Heaven

Bernhard Lang

Meeting in Heaven

Modernising the Christian Afterlife, 1600–2000

PETER LANG
Frankfurt am Main · Berlin · Bern · Bruxelles · New York · Oxford · Wien

Bibliographic Information published by the Deutsche Nationalbibliothek
The Deutsche Nationalbibliothek lists this publication in the Deutsche Nationalbibliografie; detailed bibliographic data is available in the internet at http://dnb.d-nb.de.

Cover Design and Cover Illustration:
© Olaf Gloeckler, Atelier Platen, Friedberg,
using an engraving
by Louis Schiavonetti, 1808.

ISBN 978-3-631-62000-7
© Peter Lang GmbH
Internationaler Verlag der Wissenschaften
Frankfurt am Main 2011
All rights reserved.

All parts of this publication are protected by copyright. Any utilisation outside the strict limits of the copyright law, without the permission of the publisher, is forbidden and liable to prosecution. This applies in particular to reproductions, translations, microfilming, and storage and processing in electronic retrieval systems.

www.peterlang.de

If someone wants to go to heaven, who am I to stop them?
  William Faulkner, *Requiem for a Nun* (1951)

    He was shot by a man on the run
    And she couldn't find how to push through.
    I stay, I pray
    See you in heaven far away.
    I stay, I pray
    See you in heaven one day.

        Moonlight shadow
        Mike Oldfield (text)
        Maggie Reilly (voice, 1983)

Contents

List of Figures and Tables 9

Preface 11

Acknowledgements 13

Chapter 1: From Stasis to Movement, from Loneliness to Love.
Heaven: A History (1988) in Retrospect 15

Chapter 2: The Modernisation of Life after Death, 1644–1791:
A Survey 33

Chapter 3: The English Heaven. An Exploration
of *The Pilgrim's Progress* (1678/84) 43

Chapter 4: The Spanish Heaven. Opposition to Modernity 61

Chapter 5: A Swedish Heaven. Swedenborg on *Heaven and Hell* (1758) –
Appendix: Swedenborg Chronology 79

Chapter 6: A Swedish Heaven in European Thought.
Early Readers of Swedenborg.
Appendix: Thomas Hartley on Swedenborg's Doctrine
of Correspondences (1778) 123

Chapter 7: American Heavens.
An Exploration of Cemeteries, 1740–1850 143

Index 161

List of Figures and Tables

Figures

3.1 William Blake, The Meeting of a Family in Heaven. – Robert Blair, *The Grave. Illustrated by Twelve Etchings*, London: R.H. Cromeck, 1808. 55
3.2 William Blake, Christian and Hopeful at the Gate of Heaven. – Gerda S. Norvig, *Dark Figures in the Desired Country: Blake's Illustrations to The Pilgrim's Progress*, Berkeley: University of California Press, 1993, plate 28. 57
5.1 Swedenborg's Map of the Universe (first version). 82
5.2 Swedenborg's Map of the Universe (second version). 91
7.1 Succession of gravestone designs in Stoneham cemetery, Massachusetts. – James Deetz, *In Small Things Forgotten: The Archaeology of Early American Life*, Garden City, N.Y.: Anchor Press, 1977, p. 70. 148
7.2 Winged skull and cherub. – James Deetz, *In Small Things Forgotten: The Archaeology of Early American Life*, Garden City, N.Y.: Anchor Press, 1977, p. 74. 149

Tables

5.3 Swedenborg's distinction between will and intellect 106
5.4 Swedenborg chronology 121
6.1 Wesley's comments on Swedenborg 134
7.3 Major themes in American epitaphs. – After Michel Vovelle, 'A Century and One-Half of American Epitaphs 1660–1813', *Comparative Studies in Society and History* 22 (1980), pp. 534–547, from pp. 541 and 545 151
7.4 Puritan and Victorian notions of heaven 158

Preface

Heaven, in Christianity, is the traditional name of the abode of God, the angels, saints, the blessed among the dead believers, and, eventually, redeemed humankind. The Bible locates heaven at the top of a three-tiered structure comprising netherworld (below the earth), earth, and heaven (above the sky). As a powerful symbol denoting a superior realm, this location has survived modern revisions of this archaic cosmological description. In Christian thought and language, heaven figures prominently in two traditions that may be termed 'visionary' and 'eschatological'. The visionary tradition is about the experience of some people who have reported their being admitted to heaven in dreams or visions. The eschatological tradition is about the life after death that Christians hope to spend in the abode of God.

From around 1980, Christian notions of heaven have been a focus of my research in the history of religions. This research deals with individual authors, analysing written sources and sometimes works of art, while at the same time being intent on producing a comprehensive interpretation of the immense masses of evidence by painting 'the big picture'. Detailed analysis and sweeping synthesis are the two closely related tasks of the historian. Without the broader picture, detailed analysis of individual evidence is tedious, unproductive, and ultimately irrelevant, while an overview, if not supported and illustrated by quotations from sources, names of authors, and illuminating stories, becomes abstract, dogmatic, and equally irrelevant. Working with these guidelines in mind, I was able to publish a comprehensive study entitled *Heaven: A History* (New Haven and London: Yale University Press, 1988; 2nd ed. 2001). Much to the surprise – and delight – of my co-author Colleen McDannell and myself, the echo was overwhelming. The international press hailed it as a well-written cultural history of human hope, while specialised journals acclaimed it as a major contribution to the study of Christian thought through two millennia. My German translation followed – *Der Himmel: Eine Kulturgeschichte des ewigen Lebens* (Frankfurt: Suhrkamp, 1990). Further translations appeared in Spanish, Italian, Dutch, Korean, and Japanese, and apparently also in a pirate version in Serbocroat.

Heaven: A History uses one conceptual distinction as its central interpretative tool: that between 'anthropocentric' and 'theocentric' notions of life everlasting.

When trying to find a label to characterise the view of life after death that is focused primarily or even exclusively on God, the adjective 'theocentric' suggested itself. Equally, the expectation of a celestial life that involves communality, love, work, and an environment resembling that in which we live now, demanded a label, and this was found in the term 'anthropocentric'. These two adjectives distinguish recognisable emphases in the ideas found in the many sources relevant to the study of heaven. Used as approximations and rough guides, these labels serve the analysis and help to paint the broad picture, but should of course not be used to overplay the finer points made by individual theological authors or novelists writing on heaven and the saints' activities and enjoyments. Will we be reunited with our beloved ones in eternal life? Can one expect to experience emotionally strong individual friendships in the other world? Or will heavenly existence be something very different, consisting mainly or exclusively in the vision of God? *To meet or not to meet the loved ones*: despite the finer points of theological speculation, this was the simple question that Christians often discussed.

In addition to publishing *Heaven: A History*, I have given many lectures on the subject, read papers at academic conferences, published articles, and contributed to research projects. Some of these contributions and studies have been published in one form or another; others have never been made available in print. While the idea of collecting my 'heaven' papers in one volume was never far from my mind, the project was always postponed, generally because of a busy academic teacher's lack of time and tranquillity. But the day came for a short sabbatical leave from the University of Paderborn, and I used it for reviewing my celestial collection and selecting papers that might interest others. Although I have revised much of the material in the interest of clarity, I still stand by the original arguments. Nevertheless, I came to realise that it is impossible 'to enter the same river a second time', as an ancient Greek philosopher shrewdly noted. While revising the papers, I was delighted to discover that despite their origin in different contexts, they tell one single story, justifying the subtitle 'Modernising the Christian Afterlife'.

I record with gratitude the generous help received from my favourite Scottish editor who insists on remaining anonymous. Further help came from Ursula Hennigfeld and my assistants Susanne Pramann and Tomasz Manka, and from our university photographer Adelheid Rutenburges.

Bernhard Lang
2011

Acknowledgements

1. From Stasis to Movement, from Loneliness to Love. *Heaven: A History* (1988) in Retrospect. – Unpublished. Part of this essay was used for introducing the second (2001) edition *of Heaven: A History, see* Bernhard Lang and Colleen McDannell, *Heaven: A History*, New Haven: Yale University Press, 2001, pp. xiii–xix.
2. The Modernisation of Life after Death, 1644–1791: A Survey. – Shorter version published as 'Some Baroque Ideas on Life after Death, and on Heaven and Hell' in: Emanuel Swedenborg, *Heaven and Its Wonders and Hell*. Translated by George F. Dole, West Chester, Penn.: Swedenborg Foundation, 2000, pp. 65–69.
3. The English Heaven: An exploration of *The Pilgrim's Progress* (1678/84). – Published as 'Meeting in Heaven according to John Bunyan in *The Pilgrim's Progress*. With a Note on an Illustration by William Blake' in: *Tod und Jenseits in der Schriftkultur der Frühen Neuzeit*. Edited by Marion Kobelt-Groch and Cornelia Niekus Moore (Wolfenbütteler Forschungen 119), Wiesbaden: Harrassowitz, 2008, pp. 119–135.
4. The Spanish Heaven: Opposition to Modernity. – Earlier version published in Spanish as the preface to the Spanish edition of *Heaven: A History*: Bernhard Lang and Colleen McDannell, *Historia del Cielo*. Traducción de Juan Alberto Moreno Tortuero, Madrid: Taurus, 1990, pp. 15–35.
5. A Swedish Heaven: Swedenborg on *Heaven and Hell* (1758). – Earlier version published as 'On Heaven and Hell: A Historical Introduction to Swedenborg's Most Popular Book' in: Emanuel Swedenborg, *Heaven and Its Wonders and Hell*. Translated by George F. Dole, West Chester, Penn.: Swedenborg Foundation, 2000, pp. 9–78.
6. A Swedish Heaven in European Thought: Early readers of Swedenborg. – Earlier version published as 'Some Early Readers of Heaven and Hell' in: Emanuel Swedenborg, *Heaven and Its Wonders and Hell*. Translated by George F. Dole, West Chester, Penn.: Swedenborg Foundation, 2000, pp. 49–64.
7. Heaven on Stone: American Cemeteries, 1740–1850. – Published as 'Heaven on Stone: Eighteenth- and Nineteenth-Century Ideas about Life after Death as Reflected in American Cemeteries' in: *Im Angesicht des Todes*. Edited by

Hansjakob Becker, Bernhard Einig and Peter-Otto Ullrich, St. Ottilien: Eos Verlag, 1987, vol. 1, pp. 603–619.

Chapter 1: From Stasis to Movement, from Loneliness to Love. *Heaven: A History* (1988) in Retrospect

For Colleen McDannell

Once a major research project has been completed, the results written up and published, the authors have to cut themselves free from the bondage that the matter has come to mean over the years. They have to be released and feel able to turn to something else. Yet, the enthusiastic responses of readers and reviewers of *Heaven: A History*,[1] the collaboration with translators of the book, frequent invitations to lecture on the subject to academic and other audiences in various countries (notably in the USA, in France, Austria, Germany, the Netherlands, and Denmark), and the inevitable teaching duties have kept my interest in the subject alive. During the past twenty years, my research on heaven and my thinking on the subject have not stood still.

It is especially in two areas that I would now add to or modify the text of *Heaven: A History*. First, more can be said about movement and progress in the other world, so that a more complex picture of the transformation of a static heaven into a dynamic one emerges. Second, new sources on the expectation of heavenly reunion have come to my notice. A further exploration of these two subjects can highlight what we – Colleen McDannell and myself – have termed the specifically 'modern' view of life everlasting.

The kinetic revolution in heaven

The portrayal of the shift from a static notion of heavenly existence to a dynamic view of life everlasting presents a special challenge for the researcher, because the relevant historical sources are scattered and diverse. The first notable author to state the idea of human development in the beyond was Origen (ca. 185–254).

Origen begins the relevant discussion by stating that 'there can be no living thing which can be altogether inactive and immoveable, but delights in motion of

---

1   Bernhard Lang and Colleen McDannell, *Heaven: A History*, London 1988. A second edition was published in 2001.

every kind, and in perpetual activity and volition'.[2] Activity not only characterises the present life; it will continue in the hereafter. But what kind of activity will be sustained? Origen has a clear answer: not all manner of activity will continue; only the highest-ranking activities – those of the intellect – will be eternalized. Origen defines humans as learners, for there is so much to learn and to study, both in this world and in the next. According to Origen, the soul initially spends time after the death of the body in a place that is located on earth and called 'paradise'. There it is prepared for the ascension through the various levels of the celestial spheres and for its eventual arrival at the uppermost heaven. Eric Dodds, in his celebrated *Pagan and Christian in an Age of Anxiety*, summarises Origen's view as follows: 'The good will dwell for a time in the Earthly Paradise; there God will organise a school for souls with angelic instructors, who will teach them the answers to all the questions that puzzled them on earth. Origen provides a syllabus on which the soul will eventually be examined; those who pass will be promoted to higher spheres and more advanced courses: heaven is an endless university.'[3] One may add that, according to recent opinion, Origen not only thought of angelic instructors in the hereafter; some of 'the princes and rulers, who govern those of lower rank, and instruct them, and teach them, and train them in divine things' are actually human souls who help their fellow-souls to find explanations 'for all that happens on earth', the meaning of difficult passages in Scripture, and ultimately the plan behind all the 'movements' of the universe.[4] After being promoted to a realm situated beyond the earthly paradise, the souls receive advanced instruction, apparently from Christ.[5]

In late antiquity, Origen apparently remained isolated with his bold theology of the hereafter. Although Gregory of Nyssa (ca. 331–395) asserted that the blessed individual 'will always enjoy a greater and greater participation in grace throughout all eternity',[6] his account pales in comparison with that of Origen. It was not before the late Middle Ages and the Renaissance that Christian thinkers felt encouraged to take up the subject, albeit in a different form. Some scholastic

---

2 Origen, *On the First Principles* II, 11,1 (*Sources Chrétiennes* vol. 252, p. 394).
3 Eric Dodds, *Pagan and Christian in an Age of Anxiety*, Cambridge 1965, p. 129.
4 Origen, *On the First Principles* II, 11,3 (*Sources Chrétiennes* vol. 252, p. 400). See Charles E. Hill, *Regnum Caelorum: Patterns of Future Hope in Early Christianity*, Oxford 1992, p. 130. According to Hill, Origen understood the biblical doctrine of Christ's millennial reign as referring to a post-mortem state in which the souls reigned with Christ and were at the same time trained for their further ascent to higher celestial realms.
5 See the summary in Brian E. Daley, *The Hope of the Early Church: A Handbook of Patristic Eschatology*, 2nd ed., Peabody, Mass. 2003, pp. 57–58.
6 Gregory of Nyssa, Homilies on Canticles 8 (*Patrologia Graeca*, vol. 44, col. 941).

theologians began to doubt the validity of Thomas Aquinas's biased view of the static hereafter. According to Thomas, the active life – that of worldly people who engage in worldly business – is finished with death. In the beyond, people are left with contemplation, which monks and nuns anticipate in the monastery. Denis the Carthusian (1402–1472), who lived in the monastery of Roermond in the Netherlands, comments on the matter in great detail in his treatise *On Contemplation*. Presumably inspired by the re-evaluation of the active life by Dominican mystics,[7] he concludes that there must be an 'active life' in heaven; it differs from earthly existence only in its being 'free from all imperfection' (*vita activa, utpote imperfectione omnia exclusa*).[8] Regrettably, Denis leaves the argument at that, without telling us what kind of activity he has in mind.

Denis the Carthusian's idea that the blessed actually lead an active life – a life in which work has a place – apparently was not really developed before the eighteenth century. The only idea that did become familiar earlier was that of spatial movement. *Heaven: A History* lists relevant sources from the fifteenth century,[9] but others can be added. In *The Art of Dying Well* (1619) by the Italian cardinal Robert Bellarmine (1542–1621), the Jesuit author writes: 'The seat of the blessed is most spacious. They can freely move from one place to another. And there is no danger of their becoming tired since by the gift of agility they can move from place to place in a moment.'[10] There can be no doubt about the reasoning behind the cardinal's description: since in the other world people will be transformed into angels, they will share the 'agility' (*agilitas*) – meant is mobility – generally attributed to these spiritual creatures. Elsewhere, Bellarmine explains that God gave the angels 'the power to travel at enormous speeds from heaven to earth and from earth to heaven and anywhere they wish.'[11] It is this angelic agility that the blessed share, and the very thought makes the cardinal exclaim: 'What a pleasure it will be [for the blessed] to move from the east to the west, from the south to the north, to circle the whole universe in a moment, while those who have perished remain in one place in hell for all eternity, bound hand and foot.'[12] In 1621, the English Jesuit Edward Coffin published an English

---

7   Alois M. Haas, 'Die Beurteilung der *vita contemplativa* und *activa* in der Dominikanermystik des 14. Jahrhunderts', in: *Arbeit – Musse – Meditation*. Edited by Brian Vickers, Zurich 1985, pp. 109–131.
8   Denis the Carthusian, *De contemplatione* 1:18, in: idem, *Opera omnia*, Tournai 1912, vol. 41, p. 154.
9   Lang and McDannell, *Heaven: A History*, p. 128 – Lorenzo Valla; p. 119 – Savonarola.
10 Robert Bellarmine, *De arte bene moriendi* II, 4 (*Spiritual Writings*. Edited by John P. Donnelly et al., New York 1989, pp. 334–335).
11 Bellarmine, *De ascensione mentis in Deum* IX, 4 (*Spiritual Writings*, p. 147).
12 Bellarmine, *De arte bene moriendi* II, 4 (*Spiritual Writings*, p. 335).

translation of Bellarmine's Latin *Art of Dying Well*, and in 1720, John Ball's Protestant version appeared.[13] Read by a wide clerical and lay readership, by Catholics and Protestants throughout the seventeenth and eighteenth centuries, Bellarmine's book must have shaped many people's views of life everlasting and contributed to what *Heaven: A History* calls 'the kinetic revolution of heaven'.

In Spain, Francisco Suárez (1548–1617) thought about heaven very much like his fellow-Jesuit Bellarmine. Like most theologians of his day, Suárez worked with the scholastic paradigm established by Thomas Aquinas. Suárez, however, often departed from Thomas's rigorous Aristotelianism, which emphasized the immobility of God and made the blessed the unmoving spectators of the divine. While heaven was still the empyrean, the realm that lay beyond the huge shell of the firmament, Suárez modifies the immobility of its residents. To do this, he first presents a basic structure of heaven: the blessed live on the surface of a huge sphere that encompasses the created universe as a type of solid shell. Because the heavenly world is spherical and has no mountains or other elevations, the blessed cannot see Christ from everywhere. Suárez's solution is that in heaven the blessed do not have to remain at their appointed place in eternal immobility. They can enjoy a freedom of movement just like Christ and the angels. While the souls do not as a rule descend to earth, 'because this neither belongs to their state nor to their ministry', the souls can 'move and travel in heaven itself'.[14] Suárez, following the Jesuit theology of his day, saw movement as integral to the heavenly experience. 'If one of the blessed leaves his place for a while', Suárez argues, 'why should someone else not occupy it in order to be closer to Christ or someone of the blessed?' Perhaps it was impossible for the Jesuits, whose missionary activities demanded so much travelling, to imagine a motionless heaven.

The influence of ideas such as those voiced by Bellarmine and Francisco Suárez can be documented from other seventeenth-century sources. Thus William Gearing in *A Prospect of Heaven* (1673) assured his readers that our heavenly bodies 'shall be able to move from place to place with incredible swiftness'.[15] Our present bodies are now dull and sluggish, remarked John Shower in a funerary sermon printed in London in 1693. But our heavenly bodies, he preached, 'shall be nimble and active, like the body of Christ that, at his Ascension into Heaven, being done in one day, moved many thousands of Miles between the highest Heaven and this Earth, being computed by some

---

13   John P. Donnelly in: Bellarmine, *Spiritual Writings*, p. 24.
14   Francisco Suárez, *Opera omnia*. Edited by Charles Berton, Paris 1866, vol. 19, pp. 961–962.
15   William Gearing, *A Prospect of Heaven*, as quoted in Philip C. Almond, *Heaven and Hell in Enlightenment England*, Cambridge 1994, p. 107.

hundred millions of Miles'.[16] Some time in the early eighteenth century, the American theologian Jonathan Edwards (1703–1758) included in one of his notebooks the idea that 'the saints in heaven' will employ themselves not only in 'singing God's praise, or expressing their thoughts to God and Christ, and also to one another', but also 'in going from one part of heaven and the universe to another, to behold the glories of God shining in the various parts of it'.[17] Perhaps it is justifiable to conclude that by the eighteenth century, the idea of the saints' faculty – and wish – to travel through cosmic spaces had become a familiar notion.

The 'kinetic revolution' of heaven involves more than one dimension: in addition to activity (as stated by Denis the Carthusian) and the ability to travel there is the notion of progress in the other world. *Heaven: A History* refers to the philosopher Gottfried Wilhelm Leibniz (1646–1716) as a key figure who expressed the conviction that progress is essential to celestial happiness.[18] While Leibniz does not offer further speculations, others were bold enough to do so. One of them, the German Enlightenment theologian Gottfried Less (1737–1797) seems to anticipate the thought of Charles Darwin: 'Then, in the fullness of time, a general development and exaltation may take place – stones to plants, plants to animals, animals to humans, humans to angels, angels to archangels, and so forth.'[19]

In the eighteenth century, we can see Puritan theologians struggling with the same idea and arriving at sentiments similar to those of Leibniz and other German writers. Thus Increase Mather (1639–1723) hoped that somehow the 'glorify'd souls will be still attaining unto greater degrees of knowledge'.[20] In his theological notebooks, Jonathan Edwards often comments on heaven, happiness, and the idea of progress in the other world.[21] Although this early American thinker never moved beyond writing down isolated thoughts and miniature essays, his theological vision is clear enough. Both earthly and heavenly

---

16 John Shower, *Death a Deliverance*, as quoted in Almond, *Heaven and Hell in Enlightenment England*, p. 107.
17 Jonathan Edwards, *Miscellanies*, no. 137 [152] (Jonathan Edwards, *The Works*, New Haven 1994, vol. 13, p. 295–296).
18 Lang and McDannell, *Heaven: A History*, p. 277.
19 Gottfried Less, *Christliche Religions-Theorie fürs gemeine Leben* (1779), as quoted on p. 184 of Manfred Hauke, 'Unaufhörliches Neuwerden oder restlose Erfüllung? Zur Diskussion um die visio beatifica', *Forum katholische Theologie* 7 (1991), pp. 175–195.
20 Increase Mather, *Meditations on the Glory of the Heavenly World* (1711), as quoted on p. 393 of Amy P. Paw, 'Heaven Is a World of Love: Edwards on Heaven and the Trinity', *Calvin Theological Journal* 30 (1995), pp. 392–400.
21 See Paul Ramsey, 'Heaven Is a Progressive State', in: Jonathan Edwards, *The Works*, New Haven 1989, vol. 8, pp. 706–738.

existence, for him, are dynamic states, characterised by movement and progress. Within that movement, two phases can be distinguished. The first phase, that of preparation, leads up to the end of the world and the Final Judgment. 'All things in heaven and earth, and throughout the universe, are in a state of preparation for the state of consummation; all the wheels are going, none of them stop, and all are moving in a direction to the last and most perfect state.'[22] At the consummation, 'all things come to be settled in their fixed and eternal state'.[23] While the Bible tells us much about this first phase of progress, the second phase is accessible only through theological speculation, and Edwards dares to indulge in philosophical reasoning. The 'fixed and eternal state' is not really fixed at all, but allows for further movement and progress. 'I believe the saints will be progressive in knowledge and happiness to all eternity', Edwards states in one of his notebook entries.[24] When the saints are glorified at the Last Judgment, 'the number of their ideas' is limited, but afterwards this number must be thought of as growing, for it would be absurd to suppose that they would forget 'those great and most glorious things' that they subsequently experience in 'a whole million million ages'.[25] In a more daring note, Edwards even speculates about the 'eternal progress' of heavenly love. The relevant notebook entry merits quoting in full:

> *Happiness.* How soon do earthly lovers come to an end of their discoveries of each other's beauty; how soon do they see all that is to be seen! Are they united as near as 'tis possible, and have communion as intimate as possible? How soon do they come to the most endearing expressions of love that 'tis possible to give, so that no new ways can be invented, given or received. And how happy is that love, in which there is an eternal progress in all these things; wherein new beauties are continually discovered, and more and more loveliness, and in which we shall forever increase in beauty ourselves; where we shall be made capable of finding out and giving, and shall receive, more and more endearing expressions of love forever: our union will become more close, and communion more intimate.[26]

Apparently written in 1724, when Edwards was courting his future wife Sarah Pierpont, the entry might be read as envisaging an intimate relationship between the young people that extends beyond the grave. Edwards occasionally does refer to the saints' 'special comfort in their meeting with those that were their godly friends on earth',[27] but specialists on Edwards take the entry to refer to the soul's

---

22 Edwards, *Miscellanies*, no. 435 (Edwards, *The Works*, vol. 13, p. 483).
23 Edwards, *Miscellanies*, no. 565 (Edwards, *The Works*, New Haven 2000, vol. 18, p. 104).
24 Edwards, *Miscellanies*, no. 435 (Edwards, *The Works*, vol. 13, p. 483).
25 Edwards, Miscellanies, no. 105 (Edwards, *The Works*, vol. 13, p. 275).
26 Edwards, *Miscellanies*, no. 198 (Edwards, *The Works*, vol. 13, p. 336–337).
27 Edwards, *Miscellanies*, no. 639 (Edwards, *The Works*, New Haven 2000, vol. 18, p. 170).

eternal union with God or Christ.[28] This union, which for Edwards constitutes celestial bliss, is seen as a dynamic union characterised by eternal progress, the hallmark of what may be termed the kinetic revolution of heaven.

By way of conclusion, we may add that with Jonathan Edwards begins a long line of theological authors and novelists who believed in an afterlife characterized by mobility, motion, and progress. Together with Pat Jalland, who has studied Victorian family documents and commented on the virtual absence of the idea of heavenly progress, we may suppose that the notion was 'largely confined to more progressive clergymen and Nonconformists, and [...] perhaps more influential in America' than elsewhere.[29] Progressive clergymen, especially those with an interest in philosophical reasoning, often joined the ranks of those who believed that a heaven without progress would be a rather dull place. In his 1893 manual of Catholic doctrine, the German theologian Herman Schell (1850–1906) was quite explicit on the matter.[30] Later, especially in the 1960s and 1970s, celestial stability lost ground when European theologians such as Hans Urs von Balthasar, Ladislaus Boros, and Jürgen Moltmann discovered that everlasting progress was rooted in tradition, philosophically defensible, and humanly attractive.[31]

Heavenly reunion

One of the most conspicuous expectations Christians had, and continue to have, about life after death was of being reunited with their loved ones. Even before Christianity, this expectation was quite common, for instance among the ancient Hebrews who, when dying, longed to be united to their ancestors. Their belief that this was possible is echoed in the Old Testament where we are told that 'Abraham breathed his last and died in a good old age, an old man and full of years, and was gathered to his people' (Genesis 25:8).

---

28 John E. Smith et al. (eds.), *A Jonathan Edwards Reader*, New Haven 1995, p. xxxiii. Compare Edwards, Miscellanies, no. 183 (Edwards, *The Works*, vol. 13, p. 332): 'When we feel love to anyone of the other sex, 'tis a good way to think of the love of Christ to an holy and beautiful soul.'
29 Pat Jalland, *Death in the Victorian Family*, Oxford 1999, p. 270.
30 Herman Schell, *Katholische Dogmatik*, Paderborn 1893, vol. 3/2, p. 923. For a summary of Schell's thought, see Bernhard Lang, 'Die zweigeteilte Welt: Jenseits und Diesseits in der katholischen Theologie des 19. und 20. Jahrhunderts', in: Lucian Hölscher (ed.), *Das Jenseits. Facetten eines religiösen Begriffs in der Neuzeit*, Göttingen 2007, pp. 203–232, here pp. 221–223.
31 For relevant documentation, see Hauke, 'Unaufhörliches Neuwerden'.

Abraham was no exception; all Israelites shared the notion that after death they would join their 'people' or 'fathers' in Sheol, as they called their netherworld. We know that belief in Sheol was supported and periodically called to mind in ancestor worship (later deemed unorthodox, as biblical religion developed its canonical form). However, one group departed from this doctrine and practice – the Levites. This was a guild of itinerant ritualists who specialised in the worship of Yahweh. Devoting themselves exclusively to Yahweh, they refrained from venerating their ancestors to the point of not recognising any responsibilities for kin, both living and dead.[32] Accordingly, they did not expect to be united to their ancestors after death. Instead, they were convinced that upon death, God would take them up into heaven where they would be with the Lord to whose service they had been dedicated throughout their professional lives. As one of the Levitical poets put it: let others be united to their ancestors in dark Sheol; I, a Levite, will be taken up to God. 'God will ransom my soul from the power of Sheol, for he will receive me' into heaven (Psalm 49,15). While modern readers of the Bible often take delight in the fact that psalms such as the one quoted express strong convictions about an afterlife with God, they fail to realise that the Levites thought of heavenly afterlife as a priestly privilege (which cannot be granted to the laity), and as the opposite of being reunited with one's family. According to the Levites, one cannot have both: post-mortem relationship with one's family and heavenly union with God, for the ancestors will remain forever in the netherworld, and God will remain forever in heaven. The Levites, it seems, were the first in human history to recognise two alternative kinds of afterlife – one described in terms of 'meeting one's family in the netherworld', and the other that can be summed up as 'being with God in heaven'. The distinction between the two models survived many cultural and ideological developments, even those that tended to place both God and the ancestors in celestial realms.

Heaven: A History sketches the story of both kinds of afterlife, arguing that the anthropocentric variety came into Christianity from classical antiquity. *Heaven: A History* refers to bishop Cyprian's treatise *On Mortality* (252/3) as the earliest Christian reference to heavenly reunion.[33] While bishop Cyprian of

---

32　Levitical opposition to kinship responsibilities (Deuteronomy 33:9) and ancestor worship (Psalm 16:3–4) are mentioned in the Bible. This is how the Levitical apprentice renounces ancestor worship: 'I do not prefer to you [Yahweh] the saints [= ancestors] who are in the netherworld, and cursed are all who take pleasure in them. [...] Their drink offering of blood I will not pour out or take their names on my lips' (Psalm 16:3–4, a linguistically difficult text. The last two words of v. 2 actually form the beginning of v. 3).

33　Lang and McDannell, *Heaven: A History*, p. 61. On Cyprian's treatise, see J.H.D. Scourfield, 'The De Mortalitate of Cyprian', *Vigiliae Christianae* 50 (1996), pp. 21–41.

Carthage was generally careful to distinguish between pagan and Christian ideas, he seems to have felt that Roman beliefs about post-mortem reunion were not incompatible with Christianity and, given the plague then and the fear of persecution, could be appealed to as generally held convictions. How deeply belief in heavenly reunion was already rooted in the minds of North African Christians can be seen from a text written fifty years before Cyprian composed his book *On Mortality*. This text is the *Martyrdom of Perpetua and Felicity*, and it may actually have inspired Cyprian's thought on the afterlife.

Vibia Perpetua was a twenty-two-year-old woman whom the ancient editor of the *Martyrdom of Perpetua and Felicity* introduced as 'nobly born, liberally educated, and honourably wedded'.[34] Since Perpetua refused to sacrifice for the Roman emperor's welfare and prosperity (*salus*), she was condemned to the beasts (*ad bestias*), and died a death of martyrdom in the city of Carthage in 202 or 203. Shortly before being thrown to 'a most ferocious cow, an animal not usually employed in the games',[35] and tossed to death by the beast, Perpetua wrote down her own story. While in prison she had a dream in which she saw her brother Dionocrates, who had died from a serious illness at the age of seven. In Perpetua's dream, the child was trying to drink from a heavenly well but could not reach the water. Eventually, he does reach it, and drinks from a golden cup. The *Martyrdom* explains that in heaven, Perpetua's brother drinks from the fountain of life and thus enjoys restored health. Dinocrates can then play in the other world.

The *Martyrdom of Perpetua and Felicity* also includes what may be called the prison diary of Saturus, another contemporary martyr in Carthage. Again a dream is reported, and again we read of heavenly reunion. In the dream, Saturus and Perpetua (and perhaps other martyrs) are carried up to heaven by four angels and eventually set down in a paradise garden. There they meet the martyrs Jocundus, Saturninus, and Artaxius, all of whom had been burnt alive, and Quintus, who had died in prison. It is only after meeting their friends that they are encouraged by the angels to go and greet the Lord. While meeting God is important in the account, meeting other martyrs is in fact more prominent. The scholar Jan Bremmer has suggested that the large numbers of the blessed in heaven, and their sense of community, represents an innovation in ancient thought. The Christian heaven appears crowded with the saved, in contrast with the select few that enter the Jewish hereafter or the pagan otherworld. According

---

34   *Martyrdom of Perpetua and Felicity* II,1. The most recent edition is Jacqueline Amat, *Passion de Perpétue et Félicité* (*Sources Chrétiennes* 417), Paris 1996; for an English translation, see Mareen A. Tilley, 'The Passion of Saints Perpetua and Felicity', in: Richard Valantasis (ed.), *Religions of Late Antiquity in Practice*, Princeton 2000, pp. 387–397.
35   *Martyrdom of Perpetua and Felicity* XX, 1.

to Bremmer, the idea recurs in the early Christian epitaphs, where the dead are said to have joined the *beati, iusti, electi,* and *sancti* (the blessed, the just, the elect, and the saints), 'whereas the pagan deceased of that period wander rather lonely in the Elysian fields'.[36]

The heavenly visions recorded in the *Martyrdom of Perpetua and Felicity* seem to reflect the visionary culture of the Montanist movement,[37] then a variety of Christianity prominent in North Africa. Among the Montanists, dreams and visions were seen as the continuing work of the Holy Spirit and as significant as the visions recorded in the Bible. Appreciated by the church father Tertullian between 208 and his death in ca. 225, Montanism in those days remained a movement that stayed within catholic Christianity, and we must not think of it as a sect or a separate church.[38] It may well be that the notion of heavenly reunion entered Catholic Christianity through contact with Montanism. Both Cyprian and Augustine, who were familiar with and favourable to the idea, may have inherited it from the tradition so clearly attested in our unique document, the *Martyrdom of Perpetua and Felicity*. We know from Augustine's sermons that the Christians of North Africa celebrated the feast of Saints Perpetua and Felicity on the 7th of March, a day on which the *Martyrdom* was read in public.[39] So the very text of the *Martyrdom of Perpetua and Felicity* may have been instrumental in disseminating the idea of heavenly reunion in the third, fourth, and fifth centuries. It also seems to have contributed to the idea that martyrs will ascend to heaven immediately after their death, without having to wait for the distant day of the Last Judgment and the end of human history.

In the fourth century, when theologians such as bishop Ambrose of Milan began to reflect upon the post-mortem fate of Christian emperors, this privilege of immediacy, as well as the privilege of being united with other Christians in the other world, was extended to rulers. According to Ambrose's funeral oration for emperor Valentinian II (392), the ruler's soul ascended after death and in the other world was met and embraced by his half-brother, the late emperor Gratian.[40] In his funeral oration for Theodosius I a few years later (395),

---

36   Jan N. Bremmer, *The Rise and Fall of the Afterlife*, London 2002, p. 61.
37   Jeffrey A. Trumbower, *Rescue for the Dead: The Posthumous Salvation of Non-Christians in Early Christianity*, Oxford 2001, pp. 87–89; Rex D. Butler, *The New Prophecy and 'New Visions': Evidence of Montanism in* The Passion of Perpetua and Felicitas, Baltimore, Md. 2006.
38   On the Montanist circle in early third-century Carthage, see William Tabbernee, *Montanist Inscriptions and Testimonia*, Macon, Ga. 1997, pp. 54–59.
39   Augustine, Sermons 280–282 (*Patrologia Latina*, vol. 38, pp. 1280–1286; translated in *The Martyrdom of Perpetua*, with an Introduction by Sara Maitland, Evesham 1996, pp. 49–60).
40   Ambrose, *On Valentinian* 71–72 (*Corpus scriptorum ecclesiasticorum latinorum,* vol. 73, p. 362).

Ambrose mentioned the deceased emperor's reunion with his wife and children.[41] The bishop's funeral orations were addressed to a mixed audience that included both Christians and pagans, and his references to the emperor's heavenly ascension would be heard differently by each group. Christians understood Ambrose as saying that the emperors belonged among the special dead who, like the martyrs, entered heaven immediately upon death to enjoy the company of Christ, as well as joining the community of saints. Pagans also considered emperors to belong with the special dead who enjoyed particular post-mortem privileges. For them, Ambrose's reference to heavenly ascension resonated with traditional Roman convictions about deceased emperors. Before the emperors had become Christians, i.e. before Constantine (307–337), their deaths were followed by their souls' heavenly translation and their recognition as deities by the Senate of Rome.[42] In Christian times, the formal recognition of an emperor as 'divine' was abolished, but the special, divine character of the late emperor was never doubted and continued to be a popular notion.[43] Ambrose's pagan audience must have understood his oration as a clever combination of *Scipio's Dream* and the apotheosis of the emperor.

Martyrs and the families of rulers were thus the first to inhabit the Christian heaven and to form a welcoming party for the next arrivals.

At this point, a note of caution must be sounded. That heavenly reunion figured in Christian thought in late antiquity does not mean that it actually flourished in the theological writing of this period. During the patristic period, the notion of heavenly reunion remained peripheral within the body of literature that has survived. It was only very much later, during and after the Renaissance,[44] that preachers and theologians began to consider the issue seriously. In the late seventeenth and throughout the eighteenth centuries, heavenly reunion was discussed whenever the subject of the hereafter surfaced in conversation, and by the nineteenth century, it had even found its way into popular songs.[45] While *Heaven: A History* chronicles the story in some detail, a few additional sources may be quoted to complete the picture.

---

41 Ambrose, *On Theodosius* 40 (*Corpus scriptorum ecclesiasticorum latinorum*, vol. 73, p. 392).
42 Sabine G. MacCormack, *Art and Ceremony in Late Antiquity*, Berkeley 1981, pp. 93–158.
43 On Valentinian II and Theodosius I as gods, see Manfred Clauss, *Kaiser und Gott. Herrscherkult im Römischen Reich*, Stuttgart 1999, pp. 209–215.
44 The Renaissance, with its characteristic zeal to imitate the ancients, frequently took up Cicero's idea of describing a heaven in which the great and worthy of all times meet. See Edgar Ziesel, *Die Entstehung des Geniebegriffs*, Tübingen 1926, pp. 83–89 and 179–183.
45 'They loved each other, and when they died, they hoped to be reunited some day': this refrain was heard by Madame de Staël in Meissen, Germany, a town she visited in the early nineteenth century. Germaine de Staël, *De l'Allemagne*. Edited by the Comtesse Jean de Pange, Paris 1960, vol. 5, p. 51.

One privileged moment when the notion of heavenly reunion was presumably very relevant to be uttered was that institution much valued by our Christian ancestors, but no longer in use today: the final meeting of a dying person with his or her family at the deathbed, with the uttering of last words of faith, hope, comfort, and farewell. Accounts of Puritan deathbed scenes typically give the central place to the dying individual, who was usually armed by a steadfast faith forged long before the last hour. It was sometimes reported of such saints that in their dying they gave more comfort to those present than they received. Someone's last words, ideally a well thought-out deathbed speech, were listened to with respect, transmitted within the family, and remembered whenever death was approaching.[46] One example comes from nineteen-year-old Katharine Stubbes, who died shortly after the birth of her only child in 1590. Her husband Peter Stubbes recorded his wife's last words in print: 'Oh what a comfortable [i.e., comforting] thing is this, that we shall know one another in the life to come: talk one with another, love one another, and praise God one with another.'[47] A particularly precious document is the recently published diary of Bulstrode Whitelocke (1605–1675). When the diarist's mother realised that she was about to die, she described death as 'a passage to a better life', arguing 'that they should meet again in heaven, & there partake of everlasting joyes' (1631).[48] Pronounced when returning from a visit to the doctor and not feeling well, this was not exactly a deathbed speech, but it had the same impact. After the death of Elizabeth Whitelocke, her husband, the judge James Whitelocke, 'was cheerful, yet would frequently say, that his time was butt short in this world, & that he should hasten to meet his beloved Companion in heaven, whither she was gone before, & he should soon follow after'.[49] The judge died a year after his wife, in 1632. The expectation that after death people would be reunited continued in the family line, and was shared by this couple's son, the diarist. Sailing back from Sweden in 1654, where he had been on a diplomatic mission, Whitelocke's family nearly perished in a stormy sea. During the storm, he 'encouraged his company and particularly his two sons to a submission to the will of God, & told them that if they must dye together he doubted not butt they should shortly meet together in heaven'.[50]

---

46 Ralph Houlbrooke, 'The Puritan Death-bed, c. 1560–c. 1660', in: *The Culture of English Puritanism*. Edited by Christopher Durston et al., Houndmills 1996, pp. 122–144, here p. 132; idem, *Death, Religion and the Family in England 1480–1750*, Oxford 1998, p. 170.
47 Peter Stubbes, A Christal Glasse for Christian Women (1592), quoted in Houlbrooke, *Death, Religion and the Family in England 1480–1750*, p. 45.
48 *The Diary of Bulstrode Whitelocke*. Edited by Ruth Spalding, Oxford 1990, p. 62.
49 *The Diary of Bulstrode Whitelocke*, p. 65.
50 *The Diary of Bulstrode Whitelocke*, p. 385.

While Whitelocke's diary is a private document reflecting the life and sentiments of a gentleman who was a member of the English parliament, we may briefly consider a printed work by someone from the lower classes – *The Pilgrim's Progress* by John Bunyan, a tinker by profession. When Bunyan published the second part of *The Pilgrim's Progress* in 1684, he could not avoid the subject, for 'some make a question whether we shall know one another when we are there'.[51] Bunyan of course imagined that Christian (hero of part I of *The Pilgrim's Progress*) would be joined by his wife Christiana (heroine of part II of the novel) and his four sons in the celestial city. 'Next to the joy of seeing himself there [in the celestial city], it will be a joy to meet there his wife and his children. [...] Since relations are our second self, though that state will be dissolved there, yet why may it not be rationally concluded that we shall be more glad to see them there than to see they are wanting?'[52]

A century after Bunyan and Whitelocke, the theme of 'meeting our relations' still features in English conversation, and it was familiar to Dr. Samuel Johnson, the famous English lexicographer, and his biographer James Boswell. Here is part of a 1772 dialogue between the two, as chronicled by Boswell:

> BOSWELL. One of the most pleasing thoughts is that we shall see our friends again. JOHNSON. Yes, Sir; but you must consider that when we are become purely rational, many of our friendships will be cut off. Many friendships are formed by a community of sensual pleasures: all these will be cut off. We form many friendships with bad men, because they have agreeable qualities, and they can be useful to us; but, after death, they can no longer be of use to us. We form many friendships by mistake, imagining people to be different from what they really are. After death, we shall see everyone in a true light. Then, Sir, they talk of our meeting our relations: but then all relationship is dissolved; and we shall have no regard for one person more than another, but for their real value. However, we shall either have the satisfaction of meeting our friends, or be satisfied without meeting them.[53]

In the Boswell–Johnson dialogue, the name of only one author figures – that of the Cambridge philosopher Henry More (1614–1687), who had commented on the fate of the soul in the hereafter.[54] From a review published in *The Gentleman's Magazine* of 1778 we know that another name must have occasionally featured in similar dialogues: that of the Swedish seer Emanuel Swedenborg, whose book *Heaven and Hell* was published in London in a Latin (1758) and an English edition (1778).[55]

---

51 John Bunyan, *The Pilgrim's Progress*. Edited by Roger Sharrock, Harmondsworth 1965, p. 351.
52 Bunyan, *The Pilgrim's Progress*, p. 351.
53 James Boswell, *Life of Johnson*. Edited by R.W. Chapman, Oxford 1980, p. 471.
54 On More's influence, see Almond, *Heaven and Hell in Enlightenment England*, pp. 31–37.
55 *The Gentleman's Magazine* 48 (1778), pp. 325–326 – anonymous review of Emanuel Swedenborg, *A Treatise concerning Heaven and Hell* (London 1778).

As is well known, and amply documented in *Heaven: A History*, the twentieth century saw the demise of the 'modern heaven', the hereafter characterised by anthropocentric images of reunion and cultural as well as technological progress. The new century's skepticism was well expressed in 1900 by Ernst Troeltsch, then professor of Protestant systematic theology in Heidelberg. Reflecting on the intellectual situation as a challenge for modern theology, Troeltsch also considered the subject of life after death. While he was prepared to believe in some sort of afterlife, he rejected detailed speculation: 'As for the fate of the individual beyond the world of the senses, we [theologians] have to be more restrained than earlier generations; yet, we may not give up the belief that the apparent chaos of the present age will metamorphose for us in some unknown way.'[56] The very vagueness of Troeltsch's statement was to become typical of much of twentieth-century liberal theology, both Protestant and Catholic.

This is not to say, however, that nineteenth-century ideas of heaven were quick to disappear. On the surface, academic theologians generally voice notes of restraint if not scepticism. Digging deeper into private documents of theologians such as Dietrich Bonhoeffer or Karl Rahner, however, we find that theologians have a hard time trying to move beyond traditional notions – notions that still figure prominently in people's minds, in popular religious writing, and an occasional word of the present pope.[57]

When Dietrich Bonhoeffer (1906–1945) was serving as an associate pastor in the German Protestant church of Barcelona, he faced questions that many clergy have encountered. In a letter from 1928 he reported that at eleven o'clock one

---

56 Ernst Troeltsch, *Die wissenschaftliche Lage und ihre Anforderungen an die Theologie*, Tübingen 1900, p. 55.

57 Thus Father Thomas Rosica in an article included in the 2010 Easter edition of the *Osservatore Romano*, the Vatican's semi-official newspaper, imagines a meeting of St Gianna Beretta Molla (d. 1962, canonized in 2004) with her late husband (d. 2010): 'St Gianna and her husband are now reunited in heaven and celebrate the mystery of Christ's dying and rising in the company of the Lord and his saints. I can only imagine the scene in heaven that occurred on Holy Saturday morning as this wonderful couple was reunited after forty-eight years of being apart. They would embrace their daughter Mariolina, who died as a child, and be welcomed by the Venerable Pope John Paul II who enrolled Gianna in the book of the saints.' To safeguard Catholic orthodoxy, he points out that he considers the husband a saint as well, i.e. someone who after death ascends to heaven immediately, without having to pass through purgatory. Thomas Rosica, 'A Holy Couple Reunited in Heaven', *Osservatore Romano. Weekly Edition in English* 43, no. 15 (April 14, 2010), p. 10. – In a latter of congratulation in a volume dedicated to an Augustine scholar on the occasion of this sixty-fifth birthday, P. Benedict XVI expresses the wish of one day meeting St Augustine in the other world. Guntram Förster et al. (eds.), *Spiritus et Littera: Beiträge zur Augustinus-Forschung*, Würzburg 2010, p. xvii.

morning a knock was heard at the door.[58] In came a ten-year-old boy. 'I realised that the boy, whom I knew to be quite cheerful, was different', Bonhoeffer recalled. 'All of a sudden he burst into tears, and all I could understand were the words: "Mr Wolf is dead." He continued to cry when I asked him who Mr Wolf was. It was his young German shepherd dog. He had been ill for a week, and had died no more than half an hour before.' The boy talked about the love he had for the dog, then suddenly became silent. 'But I know that he is not really dead', he concluded. 'His spirit is in heaven and has much joy.' The boy's sense of heavenly reunion had already been thrown into doubt by a schoolteacher who, when previously asked what heaven would be like, answered that she had never been there and hence did not know. 'But now please tell me whether I will see my Mr Wolf again,' the boy asked the pastor. 'He really is in heaven, isn't he?'

Bonhoeffer, who had little time to reflect, replied: 'Well, God has created both humans and animals, and there can be no doubt about his love for animals. I do believe that whoever is in a real relationship of mutual love here on earth will stay together in heaven, for to love means to be near God. How exactly this will happen, we don't know.' Bonhoeffer ends his commentary by remarking on the child's happiness and certainty on the matter. It may well be that Bonhoeffer, who at that time was studying 'Das Problem des Kindes in der Theologie' (the problem of the child in theology),[59] envied the strength of the boy's belief. Theologians, with their insistence on the primacy of God and their commitment to vagueness about the hereafter, are at once attracted to, and estranged from, the natural faith of the child.

Further insight into beliefs concerning the afterlife comes from the writings of the German Jesuit theologian Karl Rahner (1904–1984) and the Catholic author Luise Rinser (1911–2002), who exchanged letters in the 1960s, the decade of their closest association and friendship. While known for his stern opposition to all sentimental views of heavenly reunion, the Jesuit imagined in one of his love letters (for that is what they were) an everlasting home with Luise. Had not Christ himself referred to the 'many mansions' that exist in his father's kingdom?, Rahner asked his friend. Luise may have felt honoured by the thought, but her answer reads differently: 'I do not believe in such a heaven.'[60] Continuing her earlier mystical fantasies of being enveloped in God's heart, she imagined that after death she would plunge right into God's heart – not alone but

---

58 Dietrich Bonhoeffer, letter to Walter Dress, 1 September 1928 (Dietrich Bonhoeffer, *Werke*. Edited by Eberhard Bethge et al., Gütersloh 1999, vol. 17, pp. 81–84).
59 Bonhoeffer, letter to Helmut Rössler, 7 August 1928 (Bonhoeffer, *Werke*, Munich 1991, vol. 10, p. 92).
60 Luise Rinser, letter to Karl Rahner, 17 September 1962 (Luise Rinser, *Gratwanderung: Briefe der Freundschaft an Karl Rahner 1962–1984*, Munich 1994, p. 99).

accompanied by her two children and her friends, including the Jesuit. Like Perpetua, she had actually experienced this in a dream. In order to underline the centrality of her experience, she adds: 'But the beyond and the sitting at the table [of which Christ speaks], all of this we can leave to the Father's discretion. Maybe there is no beyond at all, who knows what it will turn out to be.' In the exchange between the Jesuit and his female friend, the expected roles are inverted: Luise assumes the role of the theologian who is committed to a minimalist paradigm, while Karl for a moment forgets his rationalist mind and follows the romantic inclinations of his heart.

But even the mystic withdraws at times from her rationalist and minimalist notions of heaven. Thinking of her late favourite dog Vanno, Luise felt as did the boy in Barcelona: 'I will see again my dog and all the dogs of my life, for they are part of my life, which means they will be saved together with myself, for they are immortal.'[61] In one of her letters, she confides to her Jesuit friend that in conversation with the doorkeeper of her home in Italy, she actually spoke about heavenly reunion. The conversation was apparently occasioned by All Souls' Day on 2nd November, and the doorkeeper's remark that, being an atheist, he did not believe in life after death. Luise admitted to him that she too had her difficulties with traditional Catholic beliefs. Eventually, however, she came close to uttering a word of prophecy: 'I said, "Antonio, as truly as I stand here – the two of us will meet again in heaven; this I promise you." The words came out of me with such seriousness that both of us were astonished. A strange moment [...]. The conversation we had as we were standing in the draughty corridor was very sweet, lasting as it did for about twenty minutes.'[62] Apparently, two souls were dwelling in the breast of Rahner's female correspondent: the first follows her Jesuit friend's minimalist teaching, according to which there is only God after death, for God alone suffices. Her second soul, however, prompts her to improvise a sermon of consolation followed by this almost prophetic announcement.

As the case of Karl Rahner and Luise Rinser demonstrates, there is a world of difference between what intellectuals state (and publish) as their considered opinion, and what they express in unguarded moments. When they speak as lovers, and in moments of existential involvement, they are quick to resort to the expectation of heavenly reunion. In this they share the belief of Perpetua the dreamer and the bereaved boy in Barcelona. The dreamer, the lover, and the child all share the same hope, the hope so vividly – and touchingly – portrayed

---

61 Luise Rinser, preface to Eugen Drewermann, *Über die Unsterblichkeit der Tiere*, Olten 1990, p. 17.
62 Luise Rinser, letter to Karl Rahner, 1 November 1964 (Rinser, *Gratwanderung*, p. 108).

by William Blake in his Bunyan-inspired etching 'The Meeting of a Family in Heaven' (see below, Fig. 3.1). I am unwilling to construct a wall between the person as theologian and the person as lover. Who is to judge which situation is more conducive to finding the truth: the quiet of the study when ideas can be thought out in a rational and detached manner, or the moment that prompts the spontaneous reaction of the concerned individual? For all its sophistication and brilliant argumentation, theological intellectualism with its insistence on a God-centred hereafter has never been able to erase the natural longings of the human heart.

Chapter 2: The Modernisation of Life after Death, 1644–1791: A Survey

In our generation, life after death, heaven, and hell no longer form subjects that readily arise in conversation. In the seventeenth and eighteenth centuries, people had a different attitude. Most took an interest in the matter, and not a few philosophers, theologians and – not to forget – novelists and essayists offered their thoughts on heaven in print, sometimes adding their musings on hell. Philosophers during this period often limited the discussion to 'the problem of immortality', but heaven and hell did figure in the debate. In Britain, from around 1640, and at least for one century, 'almost every aspect of the afterlife gave rise to speculation or debate among scholars'.[63] Not only in Britain, of course. One author has counted the books on immortality that were published in Germany between 1751 and 1758 and noted 54 separate works.[64] In other European countries, one would no doubt find similar figures: baroque and Enlightenment authors can be credited with the first real exploitation of the theme.

From this exploration, a new, modern portrait of the afterlife emerged, a portrait characterised by its emphasis on the human side of heaven. Although prudent authors also referred to heaven as a place in which men, women, and children did come into contact with God and Christ, they stressed that heavenly life was real *human* life, and not just a case of losing oneself in mystic meditation and adoration. This meant that there had to be reunion – emotionally charged, sentimental reunion – with one's friends and with one's partner of the opposite sex. No less important were the notions of movement, progress, and productive work in an environment that despite its lack of sin, estrangement, disappointment, war, and death, was very much like our present world. While the human heaven was appreciated in all its diversity and complexity, at least some authors (such as Isaac Watts and Emanuel Swedenborg) insisted that one should abandon traditional notions of God as consisting of three persons. They preferred to speak, quite simply, of just one Lord. This shift of focus from God to post-

---

63 Ralph Houlbrooke, *Death, Religion and the Family in England, 1480–1750*, Oxford 1998, p. 50.
64 Rudolf Unger, 'Der Unsterblichkeitsgedanke im 18. Jahrhundert und bei unseren Klassikern', *Zeitschrift für systematische Theologie* 7 (1929/30), pp. 431–460, here p. 433.

mortem humankind was considered 'modern' – a shift from esoteric speculation to practical and rational notions.

The following list of eighteen items is perhaps too brief to do full justice to early-modern writing on life after death, heaven and hell; nevertheless, it can serve to introduce the reader to some of the ideas then under discussion. It may also serve as a prologue to the more detailed study of heaven in the work of two prominent authors – John Bunyan and Emanuel Swedenborg – in chapters 3 and 5 of the present book. Bunyan stands for the seventeenth century, in which heaven was only hesitantly modernised. In Swedenborg, the more daring eighteenth century found its most accomplished explorer of the other world.

Philosophy

1. *Two Treatises* [...] *of the Immortality of Reasonable Soules* (1644). In keeping with the teaching of his church, Sir Kenelm Digby, a Catholic philosopher and scientist,[65] was convinced of the immortality of the human soul. In his philosophical interpretation of traditional Christian thought he came to deny the existence of divine judgment. He argued that 'if a man die in disorderly affection to anything as to his chief good, he eternally remains, by the necessity of his own nature, in the same affection; and there is no imparity that, to eternal sin, there should be imposed eternal punishment'.[66] A century later, Swedenborg would describe everlasting existence in hell in the same way (below, no. 10).

2. *The Immortality of the Soul* (1659). The Cambridge philosopher Henry More, well known as a follower of Plato, offered much more than the title of his book seems to indicate. Like other Platonists of his time, he tried to avoid a strict separation between the spiritual and the material worlds, seeing the spiritual aspect as part of the universe as we know it. For the seventeenth-century Platonists, explains the historian Philip Almond, 'no great gulf was fixed between the living and the dead'.[67] Both the living and the dead belonged to the same spatio-temporal realm, with angels, the blessed, and God placed in the higher regions, and the wicked souls and Satan in the air around the earth and in the cavities within the earth.[68] At times, the souls of the blessed 'sing and play and dance together, reaping the lawful pleasures of the very animal life, in a far

---

65 Philip C. Almond, *Heaven and Hell in Enlightenment England*, Cambridge 1994, pp. 70–71.
66 Kenelm Digby, *Two Treatises* [...] *of the Immortality of Reasonable Soules*, Paris 1644, p. 445.
67 Almond, *Heaven and Hell in Enlightenment England*, p. 36.
68 Almond, *Heaven and Hell in Enlightenment England*, p. 36–37.

higher degree than we are capable of in this world'.[69] According to More, the souls retain certain feminine and masculine features.[70] For a long time to come, More's work was not forgotten – Dr. Johnson mentioned it in a conversation with James Boswell in 1772.[71]

3. *Systema theologicum* (Theological System, 1686). In this manuscript the famous philosopher and mathematician Gottfried Wilhelm Leibniz argued that the spiritual state in which someone dies actually determines his or her fate in the spiritual world. 'Whenever a soul leaves the body in the state of mortal sin, i.e., being ill-affected toward God, it falls as it were automatically into the abyss of hell, just like a heavy thing which is broken off and not held back by some external agent. Estranged from God, it imposes damnation upon itself.'[72] Human souls 'obviously continue to follow the path which they have begun and stay in the spiritual state in which they died.'[73] While this document was not edited until the nineteenth century, it nevertheless demonstrates that one of Swedenborg's teachings (see below, no. 10) was within the range of baroque thought.

4. *Kritik der praktischen Vernunft* (Critique of Practical Reason, 1788). Throughout his career as a philosopher, Immanuel Kant struggled with the traditional Christian doctrine of life after death. In his lectures on *Allgemeine Naturgeschichte und Theorie des Himmels* (A Natural History and Theory of Heaven, 1755), he affirmed that human beings have immortal souls. After death, souls can leave the earth to ascend to other planets where they may spend life everlasting. Later, Kant rejected this flight of fantasy, suggesting a less speculative conception. In *Träume eines Geistersehers* (Dreams of a Spirit-Seer, 1766) he argued against Swedenborg's heavenly descriptions, and in *Kritik der praktischen Vernunft* he declared immortality to be a meaningful and indeed necessary hypothesis of moral philosophy, but claimed that this hypothesis cannot be used to extend our knowledge. Immortality belongs to philosophical faith, but not to theoretical knowledge. We must refrain from speculating about the details of eternal life.

---

69 Henry More, *The Immortality of the Soul*, London 1659, p. 420.
70 Lang and McDannell, *Heaven: A History*, p. 212; Almond, *Heaven and Hell in Enlightenment England*, p. 31.
71 James Boswell, *Life of Johnson* [1791]. Edited by R.W. Chapman, Oxford 1980, p. 471.
72 Gottfried Wilhelm Leibniz, *Theologisches System*. Edited and translated by C. Haas, Hildesheim 1966, p. 193.
73 Leibniz, *Theologisches System*, p. 9.

Theology

5. *Von den vier letzten Dingen: nämlich von dem Tod, Gericht, Hölle und Himmelreich* (On the Four Last Things: Death, Judgment, Hell, and the Kingdom of Heaven, 1680). Written by the Capuchin friar Martin of Cochem and appended to his *Großes Leben Christi* (Large Life of Christ), this work introduced baroque Catholics to a very sensuous otherworld. For him, heaven 'is not something spiritual as some suppose, but something corporeal, made of some kind of matter and having form and substance'.[74] He refers to 'a real river, real trees, real fruit, and real flowers that please our vision, taste, smell, and touch in unsurpassable ways'.[75] Friar Martin's often reprinted work exemplifies German baroque preaching and spiritual writing.

6. *A Vindication of the Immortality of the Soul and a Future State* (1703). William Assheton, rector of Beckenham in Kent, sought to refute the idea that heavenly life consisted in 'bare speculation, gazing upon each other, and admiring each other's perfections'.[76] In heaven, people will lead an active life. God's Kingdom will have 'laws and statutes and governors and subjects, and those of different ranks, orders, and degrees'.[77]

7. *Death and Heaven; or the Last Enemy Conquered, and Separate Spirits Made Perfect* (1722). Isaac Watts, author of hymns ('O God, Our Help in Ages Past') and minister of an independent church in London, describes a heaven full of movement and life. The blessed will serve God 'perhaps as priests in his temple, and as kings, or viceroys, in his wide dominions'.[78] His examples of heavenly employments include the reporting of the 'faithful execution of some divine commission' and ruling 'over inferior ranks of happy spirits' or over 'whole provinces of intelligent beings in lower regions'.[79] Although not mentioned in *Death and Heaven*, Watts also questioned traditional notions of the Trinity (see

---

74 Martin von Cochem, 'Von den vier letzten Dingen: nämlich von dem Tod, Gericht, Hölle und Himmelreich', in: idem, *Das große Leben Christi*, Mariazell 1753, appendix, pp. 165–166.
75 Martin, 'Von den vier letzten Dingen', p. 170.
76 William Assheton, *A Vindication of the Immortality of the Soul and a Future State*, London 1703, p. 57.
77 Assheton, *A Vindication of the Immortality of the Soul*, p. 58.
78 Isaac Watts, 'The Happiness of Separate Spirits' [1722], in: idem, *Works*, London 1812, vol. 2, pp. 374–442, here pp. 398–399. This is 'discourse two' of a series titled 'Death and Heaven; or The Last Enemy Conquered, and Separate Spirits Made Perfect; With an Account of the Rich Variety of Their Employments and Pleasures'.
79 Watts, 'The Happiness of Separate Spirits', pp. 402–403.

also below, no. 10). *Death and Heaven* had been through four editions by 1737, and sixteen by 1818.

8. *Festum Magnum* (The Great Feast-Day, 1724, Swedish). Jesper Swedberg (since his ennoblement in 1719, Swedenborg), Lutheran bishop of Skara in central Sweden and father of Emanuel Swedenborg, was a prolific author. Some of his devotional books, all written in Swedish, include references to heaven and heavenly life. In *Festum Magnum* he writes about the interest the blessed have in the life of their earthly relatives. In another book, *Sanctificatio Sabbati* (Observing the Sabbath, 1734), he offers his views of how the blessed in heaven talk to each other: although everyone uses his or her native language, everyone understands the others. Although the bishop does not seem to have offered any sustained descriptions of the other life, his writings betray interest in the subject and the ease with which it could surface in baroque preaching.[80]

9. *Eternity of Hell Torments* (1730s). Jonathan Edwards, the foremost theologian of eighteenth-century New England, planned to write a 'rational account' of Christianity, a treatise meant to demonstrate its thoroughly rational character. Edwards never wrote this treatise, but his papers include many notes on the project, some of which refer to heaven and hell. The note on 'hell torments' asks why it is that sinners will be punished in hell eternally, although, rationally considered, each sin deserves only punishment for a limited time period. The solution is this: 'The wicked, when they are cast into hell, will continue sinning still. Yea, they will sin more than ever; their wickedness will be unrestrained.' Accordingly, God must inflict ever new punishment, 'and so on in infinitum'.[81]

10. *De Coelo et ejus mirabilibus et de inferno* (Heaven and Its Wonders and Hell, 1758). Emanuel Swedenborg published this book anonymously and in Latin, but subsequently it became available in English and many other translations, and proved to be the most influential eighteenth-century treatise on life after death. The following assertions and claims captured the attention of early readers immediately: there is only one divine person, not three (Swedenborg rejects traditional Christian teachings about the Trinity); there is no formal divine judgment of those who have died, because after death, someone's good or evil character asserts itself and determines his or her eternal state in

---

80 Martin Lamm, *Swedenborg. Eine Studie über seine Entwicklung zum Mystiker und Geisterseher.* Translated by I. Meyer-Lüne, Leipzig 1922, pp. 5–6.
81 Jonathan Edwards, *The 'Miscellanies' (Entry Nos. 501–832).* Edited by Ava Chamberlain (The Works of Jonathan Edwards 18), New Haven 2000, p. 113 (no. 574).

heaven or hell; marriage and social life continue in heaven. Moreover, 'all children, whether born inside or outside the church, are adopted by the Lord and become angels'.[82] Swedenborg claims to have acquired all his information via visionary contact with angels, i.e. former men and women who have become angels after death. Swedenborg describes a special breathing technique that enabled him to make contact with the angelic world.[83]

11. *Aussichten in die Ewigkeit* (Prospects of Eternity, 1768–1778). The author of this work, Johann Caspar Lavater, was Reformed minister in Zurich, Switzerland, and ranked as a celebrity known to Moses Mendelssohn and Goethe. In eternal life, he claimed, 'we will have bodies, live in corporeal worlds, will have to deal with material, sensual objects, and form one or more societies'.[84] By the time that this was written, Lavater may have become acquainted with the work of Swedenborg.[85] In 1772, Goethe reviewed the *Aussichten* in *Frankfurter Gelehrte Anzeigen*.[86]

Novels

12. *The Pilgrim's Progress* (1678, 1684). This Puritan bestseller is still considered one of the most significant works of English literature. In the second part of the *Pilgrim's Progress*, John Bunyan included a discussion of the joy his protagonist Christian must feel when he is joined by his wife Christiana and their

---

82 Emanuel Swedenborg, *Heaven and Its Wonders and Hell*. Translated by George F. Dole, West Chester, Penn. 2000, p. 321 (no. 416).
83 Swedenborg, *The Spiritual Diary*, New York 1978, vol. 3, pp. 70–71 (no. 3464). See the discussion in Lars Bergquist's introduction to *Swedenborg's Dream Diary*, West Chester, Penn. 2001, pp. 51–52.
84 Johann Caspar Lavater, *Aussichten in die Ewigkeit*. 2nd ed. Hamburg, 1773, vol. 3, p. 93.
85 For Lavater's knowledge of Swedenborg's work, see Alfred Acton, *The Letters and Memorials of Emanuel Swedenborg*, Bryn Athyn, Penn. 1955, vol. 2, pp. 641–643 and Ernst Benz, 'Swedenborg und Lavater', *Zeitschrift für Kirchengeschichte* 57 (1938), pp. 153–216. Benz (pp. 155–156) speculates that Lavater was largely inspired by Swedenborg, having in vain tried to contact the latter in order to solicit Swedenborg's opinion of his books. He also asked for information about a dead friend. Lavater seems to have avoided acknowledging his indebtedness to Swedenborg because of Immanuel Kant's critique in *Dreams of a Spirit Seer* (1766).
86 Johann Wolfgang Goethe, 'Review of *Aussichten in die Ewigkeit*' [1772], in: idem, *Sämtliche Werke. Münchener Ausgabe*. Edited by K. Richter, Munich 1987, vol. 1/2, p. 384.

sons in the celestial city.[87] Those who read both parts of the *Pilgrim's Progress* will detect a shift from a purely 'theocentric' heaven in the first part to 'anthropocentric' notions in the second. Bunyan's book marks the shift from general acceptance of one model to the other. Subsequently, 'meeting again in heaven' became an idea frequently invoked in sentimental novels.

13. *Julie, ou La Nouvelle Héloïse* (The New Eloïse, 1761). This long sentimental novel is about the love between Saint-Preux (a teacher) and Julie (a noble lady). The two cannot marry because Julie's father has promised her hand in marriage to Monsieur de Wolmar, and there is no way of preventing this outcome. Saint-Preux and Julie stay in touch, and for some time, Saint-Preux lives in her household. Julie's sense of virtue precludes any love affair. Julie eventually dies after rescuing one of her boys who had fallen into a lake. In her last letter to Saint-Preux, she reaffirms her love for him, and expresses the conviction that in the next world, they will eventually be united. There, she will belong to him rather than to Wolmar. '*La vertu qui nous sépara sur la terre nous unira dans le séjour eternel. Je meurs dans cette douce attente*' (the virtue that has separated us on earth will unite us in the eternal abode. I die in this sweet expectation).[88]

14. *Emile, ou De l'Education* (Emile, or On Education, 1762). Jean-Jacques Rousseau's treatise on education includes a famous chapter on religion, generally known as 'the profession of faith of the Savoyard vicar' (book IV). Although this text does not comment specifically on eschatological subjects, it rejects traditional notions about hell. According to these notions, unbaptised children who died in early infancy would eternally suffer in hell. Rousseau's Savoyard discusses and rejects this opinion: 'We hold that no child who dies before the age of reason will be deprived of eternal happiness'.[89] For opinions and debates about this subject, see above, no. 10, and below, no. 17.

15. *Die Leiden des jungen Werthers* (The Sorrows of Young Werther, 1774). This is Johann Wolfgang von Goethe's anonymously published epistolary novelette that plunged the whole of Europe into tears. The story is told of a young man who broods over his hopeless love for a married woman until he

---

87 John Bunyan, *The Pilgrim's Progress*. Edited by R. Sharrock, Harmondsworth 1965, p. 351. See below, Chapter 3, in the present book.
88 Jean-Jacques Rousseau, *Oeuvres complètes*. Edited by Bernard Gangebin and Marcel Raymond (Bibliothèque de la Pléiade), Paris 1964, vol. 2, p. 743.
89 Jean-Jacques Rousseau, *Emile, or On Education*. Translated by A. Bloom, London 1991, p. 258.

finally commits suicide. In his farewell-letter to Lotte, Werther expresses the conviction that she would eventually join him in heaven where they would spend everlasting life in 'an eternal embrace' (*ewige Umarmungen*) under the benign eye of God. The book was a bestseller. It is interesting to compare Goethe's story with Rousseau's *Julie* (above, no. 13): Goethe has a male, not a female protagonist, and he dies not through an accident but commits suicide; the expectation of meeting the desired partner in the other world is the same.

Essay, letters, and biography

16. *The Spectator,* no. 111, July 7, 1711. This issue of London's famous *Spectator*, one of the 'moral dailies' in which Enlightenment authors sought to disseminate their views among the educated, is dedicated to 'the Immortality of the Soul'. The essayist Joseph Addison rejected the unchanging character of sainthood, arguing that there must be movement and progress in the hereafter. God presents us with only the 'rudiments of existence here, and afterwards [we will] be transplanted into a more friendly climate, where they may spread and flourish to all eternity'.[90] Addison does not describe heaven. In a later issue of the *Spectator*, John Hughes refers to Cicero's dialogue *On Old Age* in which Cato looks forward to meeting his friends and ancestors in the other world.[91] Emanuel Swedenborg (see above, no. 10) may have read the *Spectator* during one of his early stays in Britain.[92]

17. *The Gentleman's Magazine* 9, 1739. This famous monthly publication not only chronicles and comments on current events, but also includes a correspondence section in which readers, often under pen-names, express themselves freely on the subject of their choice. In the January number a 'Theophilus' complains of authors who, following John Milton's *Paradise Lost*, are 'corrupting our Notions of Spiritual Things, and sensualizing our Ideas of Heaven to a Degree that may have ill Effects on Religion in general: It is letting Fancy obtrude its wild Luxuriance into the Place of Truth and Reason, and making room for the grossest and most absurd kind of Enthusiasm, and if one is

---

90 Joseph Addison, [untitled essay] in: *The Spectator* no. 111, July 7, 1711 (*The Spectator*. Edited by D.F. Bond, Oxford 1965, vol. 1, pp. 456–459, here p. 458).
91 John Hughes, [untitled essay], in: *The Spectator* no. 537, November 15, 1712 (*The Spectator*. Edited by D.F. Bond, vol. 4, pp. 416–420).
92 See the editor's note in Swedenborg, *The Spiritual Diary*. Translated by G. Bush and J. Buss, New York 1978, vol. 4, p. 457 (no. 5565).

to interpret his [i.e., Milton's] other Descriptions of Heaven by this Hint, it is every whit as sensual as the Mahometan's'.[93] In the April issue of the same year, 'Cleomenes' asks readers to discuss the afterlife of infants who die at an early age, suggesting that their souls are either annihilated after death, or that they transmigrate into other bodies again.[94] Beginning with the January number of the *Gentleman's Magazine* 1740, the editor included many responses to 'Cleomenes'[95] 'G.F.', the first contributor to the debate, insisted that any solution should be based on 'Reason guided by Revelation'.[96]

18. *Life of Samuel Johnson* (1791). James Boswell records a conversation he had with Dr. Johnson on Sunday, 28 March 1772. The subject was eternal life. After death, says Johnson, many friendships will no longer exist, for 'we form many friendship by mistake, imagining people to be different from what they really are. After death, we shall see every one in a true light'.[97] Here Johnson alludes to the New Testament: St. John says of the Lord, 'we shall see him as he is' (1 John 3:2), and the notion is readily applicable to others as well. More important than the various theories about life everlasting that surface in the conversation is the very fact that the subject comes up so naturally. The beginning of the conversation between Boswell and Johnson fits the conclusion of our survey. Boswell: 'But, Sir, is there any harm in our forming to ourselves conjectures as to the particulars of our happiness, though the scripture has said but very little on the subject?' Johnson: 'Sir, there is no harm.'[98]

---

93 *The Gentleman's Magazine* 9 (1739), p. 5b.
94 *The Gentleman's Magazine* 9 (1739), pp. 177–179.
95 *The Gentleman's Magazine* 10 (1740), pp. 3–4, 52–54, 167–168, 145–146, 341–342, 441–443; see Houlbrooke, *Death, Religion and the Family in England*, pp. 52–53.
96 *The Gentleman's Magazine* 10 (1740), p. 4b.
97 James Boswell, *Life of Johnson* [1791]. Edited by R.W. Chapman, Oxford 1980, p. 471.
98 Boswell, *Life of Johnson*, p. 471.

Chapter 3: The English Heaven. An Exploration of *The Pilgrim's Progress* (1678/84)

Seventeenth-century England boasted numerous religious talents, and even today no historian writing on this period fails to mention at least three outstanding theological thinkers: John Milton (1608–1674), Richard Baxter (1615–1691), and John Bunyan (1628–1688). Baxter and Bunyan, both coming from humble families, form a duo. Baxter was the son of a small landowning peasant, Bunyan's father was a tinker. Both became leading personalities in religious circles without ever having attended university; their education was largely autodidactic. As nonconformists, both disagreed with the established Church of England, and accordingly suffered from repressive measures and persecution by the state; both, moreover, spent considerable periods in prison. John Milton differs from the others in that he was born into a socially privileged family. Educated at St. Paul's school in London and at Christ's College, Cambridge, he was a man of considerable learning. Like the others, his religious persuasions were nonconformist, and, again like the others, he was not spared a term in prison.

Today, all three of the theologians still have a circle of followers and admirers who cultivate their work and thought. Some of the writings of Baxter enjoy much prestige among conservative Reformed theologians and church people; they are reprinted and read as classics. John Bunyan came to world fame through his novel *The Pilgrim's Progress*; read until the twentieth century as a book of devotion, it ranks as a classic of English literature. It is often asserted that, next to the Bible, *The Pilgrim's Progress* is the world's most widely read book. The number who read John Milton's long epic *Paradise Lost* is certainly much smaller than the readership of Bunyan, though historians of literature, who rediscovered Milton's work in the eighteenth century, value it more highly than that of Bunyan. In *Paradise Lost*, Milton created the most important epic in English; even today, it is read in every British institution of higher education just as in Germany all pupils have to study Goethe's *Faust*. The achievements of our three theologians may be summarised by saying that Baxter became a Puritan church father, while Milton and Bunyan are respected and revered figures in the history of English literature. But when considered as Christian teachers, they have to be grouped differently: Bunyan and Baxter teach a relatively orthodox Christian theology in the Puritan tradition originally nourished by John Calvin.

Milton, by contrast, is leaning towards free and unorthodox positions; his independence of traditional Christian teachings is evident from much of his work.

More than two decades ago I had the opportunity of studying seventeenth-century theology. The focus of my interest was the ideas that Christians, their preachers and theological teachers had about life everlasting.[99] As I delved into the writings of Milton and Baxter, I quickly found what I was looking for – and was surprised how much they differed in their views of heaven. I relied for Richard Baxter on *The Saints' Everlasting Rest* (1649), a voluminous work not to be confused with its numerous abridgements mostly printed in the nineteenth century. Baxter had little difficulty in filling more than 800 pages, although his message is quite simple and straightforward: in life everlasting, the redeemed are focussed on God alone, for he is the source of all their bliss. Social life in heaven rarely comes into view, and when the subject happens to come up, Baxter is quick to give it a theocentric turn. In the work of Milton, however, we see the beginning of a radically anthropocentric notion of heaven: the after-world as a realm designated for men and women, indeed a world of intra-human love and desire that may culminate in exclusive relationships and erotic fulfilment. In Baxter's book, there is none of this: he cannot conceive of heaven other than in strictly theocentric notions. His interest in congregational singing is particularly well expounded. Through singing, earthly congregations practice for the never-ending song of praise that they will offer to glorify God in eternity.

Milton presents a radically different picture. In *Paradise Lost* (1667) the focus is on the marital union: neither the paradise of Adam and Eve nor the realm of the angels can be thought of as lacking tenderness and erotic love. This is his point of departure. However, he does not actually tell us how he imagines life everlasting to be – which is understandable for someone who thinks of the human soul as dissolving together with the body at death, in order to be called back into being only at the Last Judgement. Then and then only will a decision be made about someone's eternal destiny in bliss or in torment, in heaven or hell. I do not doubt that Milton thought of heaven as a place where the blessed are reunited with their loved ones, even though the poet was never explicit on this point. If we consider the history of heaven as the concept developed after Milton, he appears as a precursor to those who promoted the anthropocentric notion that came to fruition in the eighteenth and nineteenth centuries. Milton's line of thought only had to come to the notice of one Emanuel Swedenborg for it to be liberated from its traditional salvation-historical framework by the rejection of

---

99 Bernhard Lang and Colleen McDannell, *Heaven: A History*, New Haven 1988; 2nd., revised edition 2001.

the doctrine of a Last Judgment. Instead there would be an almost immediate transition from this life into a different, post-mortem existence, characterised by the reunion of lovers, the continuation of the marital bond, and indeed of continuing conjugal pleasures. All of this was somehow implied in Milton's poetry; Swedenborg made it explicit and developed it into a new body of doctrine.

And as for Bunyan: what is his heaven like? In fact, one would expect from a seventeenth-century nonconformist a theocentric heaven not much different from the one depicted by Richard Baxter. The first volume of *The Pilgrim's Progress* actually seems to point in this direction.

The Pilgrim's Progress

The first part of Bunyan's work, published in 1678, tells the exemplary biography of 'Christian', i.e. the archetypal Christian man. He is introduced as someone who studies the Bible. His reading however makes him desperate, for he takes the message of the good book to be one of damnation. He and all fellow inhabitants of the huge and populous city are under the threat of damnation. Its name, City of Destruction, means it is destined for destruction, and this is one of the very many allegorical names characteristic of Bunyan's novel. Christian lives in the city of the damned. Converted to faith in God, he opens his heart to his wife and children, but none of them listen to him, for none is able to understand. So he takes to the road, to flee the city: 'The man began to run. Now he had not run far from his own door, but his wife and children perceiving it began to cry after him to return: but the man put his fingers in his ears, and ran on, crying, "Life, life, eternal life". So he looked not behind him, but fled towards the middle of the plain.'[100] As is quite evident, words of Jesus have inspired this scene: 'Verily, I say unto you, There is no man that hath left house, or parents, or brethren, or wife, or children, for the kingdom of God's sake, who shall not receive manifold more in this present time, and in the world to come life everlasting.'[101]

Two neighbours run after him, catch up with him and try to turn his heart. In conversation with them, Christian portrays the eternal life he aspires to:

---

100 John Bunyan, *The Pilgrim's Progress*. Ed. by Roger Sharrock, Harmondsworth 1965, p. 41. Pages 29–207 give the text of vol. 1 (1678), pp. 209–373 the text of vol. 2 (1684) of the original two-part novel.
101 Luke 18:29–30.

> There is an endless Kingdom to be inhabited, and everlasting life to be given us; that we may inhabit that Kingdom for ever. [...] There are crowns of glory to be given us; and garments that will make us shine like the sun in the firmament of heaven. [...] There shall be no more crying, nor sorrow; for he that is owner of the place will wipe all tears from our eyes. [...] There we shall be with Seraphims, and Cherubims, creatures that will dazzle your eyes to look on them. There also you shall meet with thousands, and ten thousands that have gone before us to that place; none of them are hurtful, but loving, and holy, every one walking in the sight of God and standing in his presence with acceptance for ever; in a word, there we shall see the elders with their golden crowns; there we shall see the holy virgins with their golden harps. There we shall see men that by the world were cut in pieces, burnt in flames, eaten of beasts, drowned in the seas, for the love that they bare to the Lord of the place, all well, and clothed with immortality, as with a garment. [...] The Lord, the governor of that country, hath recorded that in this book, the substance of which is, if we be truly willing to have it, he will bestow upon us freely.[102]

To be sure: there are people in this heaven – thousands upon thousands – but rather than forming a human society, they form a circle around God, the heavenly Lord. From him they receive a loving gesture: it is he (and not an angel or one of the blessed) who is wiping away their tears. What Bunyan describes is the theocentric heaven of the book of Revelation. Only one of the groups mentioned by Bunyan, the holy virgins with their harps, are not in Scripture; in the biblical text it is the elders themselves who are the music makers.[103] Here, as he often does, Bunyan enlivens the scriptural account by adding idyllic details. Later, as the story of Christian's pilgrimage continues, the theocentric image of heaven does not change. At one point, he declares to Charity, Prudence and Piety (the names of three delightful women he meets in a pilgrims' hostel): 'I would fain to be where I shall die no more, and with the company that shall continually cry, Holy, Holy, Holy.'[104] In conversation with the three women the subject of his family comes up, and Christian admits that he left them back in the City of Destruction. Asked about his wife and four children, Christian is reduced to tears, for he loves them dearly and did his best to convert them. Charity offers a word of consolation: he has tried everything he could to persuade them to join him on the pilgrimage; he cannot be held responsible for their damnation. Charity argues thus: 'If thy wife and children have been offended with thee for this they thereby show themselves to be implacable to good; and thou hast delivered thy soul from their blood.'[105] This brings the conversation to an end, and the journey continues. We do not have to go into all the adventures in store for Christian along the way, but some of the locations may be mentioned for

---

102 Bunyan, *The Pilgrim's Progress*, pp. 44–45.
103 Revelation 5:8.
104 Bunyan, *The Pilgrim's Progress*, pp. 83–84.
105 Bunyan, *The Pilgrim's Progress*, p. 85.

their famous metaphorical names: the Slough of Despond, the hill called Difficulty, the Vanity Fair, and Doubting Castle.

Near the end of the first volume, having reached the end of his earthly travels, our saintly pilgrim dies, his death being depicted as the transition to another world. As Christian dies he is not alone; he is accompanied by another pilgrim, a man named Hopeful. On reaching the other side, the two are welcomed by angels who sound their trumpets. Two luminous angelic figures escort them to the celestial city. On their way, they receive instruction about their new, heavenly existence. The question, 'What must we do in the holy place?', receives the following, somewhat predictable answer:

> You must there receive the comfort of all your toil, and have joy for all your sorrow; you must reap what you have sown, even the fruit of all your prayers, and tears, and sufferings for the King by the way. In that place you must wear crowns of gold, and enjoy the perpetual sight and visions of the Holy One, *for there you shall see him as he is* [1 John 3:2]. There also you shall serve him continually with praise, with shouting and thanksgiving, whom you desired to serve in the world, though with much difficulty, because of the infirmity of your flesh. There your eyes shall be delighted with seeing and your ears with hearing the pleasant voice of the Mighty One.[106]

This is the theocentric heaven that we have already met: eternal life in God's presence and of never-ending songs of praise. Yet, the sharpness of the theocentric focus is softened a little as the passage continues:

> There you shall enjoy your friends again, that are got thither before you; and there you shall with joy receive, even every one that follows into the holy place after you. There also you shall be clothed with glory and majesty, and put into an equipage fit to ride out with the King of Glory.[107]

So there is meeting again in heaven! Reunion with old friends! But the subject is elaborated no further. In the very next sentence, the two newcomers are promised new clothing, comparable to the attire of royal equerries riding out with their lord. After this instruction, the newcomers are guided through the gate into the heavenly city, again being welcomed with music and the solemn sound of church bells. As the gate is closed behind Christian and Hopeful, the heavenly host can be heard shouting: 'Holy, Holy, Holy, is the Lord.'[108] Thus the pilgrimage of our hero ends, and the edified reader can lay aside the book.

Originally, Bunyan had not considered the writing of a second volume of *The Pilgrim's Progress*. Bunyan's next book – *The Life and Death of Mr. Badman* (1680) – reads like a long extra chapter or appendix to the first volume of *The*

---

106 Bunyan, *The Pilgrim's Progress*, p. 201.
107 Bunyan, *The Pilgrim's Progress*, p. 201.
108 Bunyan, *The Pilgrim's Progress*, p. 202.

Pilgrim's Progress. Mr. Badman is the exact opposite to Christian. This well-respected and successful shopkeeper, inwardly corrupt and sinful, stays in the City of Corruption and belongs with the reprobate. While Christian, who fled that city, eventually entered the celestial gate, Mr. Badman ends up in hell, as was to be expected. The subject now seemed exhausted. But *The Pilgrim's Progress* turned out to be a bestselling book, with five editions printed by 1680, and Bunyan felt that a sequel might be equally successful. He wrote that sequel, and it was published in 1684, six years after the first volume. The title remains the same: *The Pilgrim's Progress*, but the subtitle explains the new plot: 'The Second Part [...] wherein is set forth the manner of the setting out of Christian's Wife and Children, their Dangerous Journey, and Safe Arrival at the Desired Country.' If Bunyan had just repeated the travel adventures of part one with variations, he would have appeared as a second-rate author. He demonstrated his skill by writing a new story, one marked once again by sensibility.

From the outset, Christiana and her four sons are accompanied by Mercy, a girl from the neighbourhood who joins them, offering her services as a maid. The dangerous journey is replaced by a kind of pleasure trip, although dramatic incidents are not lacking. The family never fails to be received into welcoming hostelries. Like tourists, they visit the places where Christian fought against, and conquered, all kinds of monsters. When it comes to a conflict, a hero does the fighting for our travelling group; this hero, Great-heart by name, accompanies them, always ready to spring to their defence. He is the exemplary knight who is always at hand when the weak are in distress, and he easily overcomes all enemies. Thus protected, the journeying group proceeds without undue haste. There is even enough time for the wedding of each of the four sons, now adults, so that the family group is extended through the addition of several women. Matthew marries Mercy the maid, and we learn that Mercy is soon with child. Christiana's other three sons meet their spouses along the way: James marries Phoebe, Samuel decides on Grace, and Joseph selects Martha for his spouse. While almost all the figures in part one of *The Pilgrim's Progress* remain without first names, these now become the mark of a certain kind of domesticity that makes us almost forget the inevitable problems of travelling, for our attention is caught up more by the descriptions of the stations and welcoming hostelries than by the journey's actual progress.

How is eternal life portrayed in this second part of the novel? Right at the beginning, when Christian's wife lives through the agonies of her own conversion, she sees a heavenly scene in a dream:

> And she thought she saw Christian her husband in a place of bliss among many immortals, with an harp in his hand, standing and playing upon it before one that sat on a throne with a rainbow about his head. She saw also as if he bowed his head with his face to the paved-work

that was under the Prince's feet, saying, 'I heartily thank my Lord and King for bringing me into this place.' Then shouted a company of them that stood round about, and harped with their harps: but no man living could tell what they said, but Christian and his companions.[109]

The celestial scene witnessed by Christiana is no less than the immediate sequel to the end of part one of *The Pilgrim's Progress*: after Christian has been received into heaven, he is given a harp, and now plays it in the grand orchestra that unites all the blessed ones. The liturgical theocentrism of the book of Revelation remains unchanged. However, we would not do full justice to Bunyan's narrative if we did not venture to move beyond this interpretation. As soon as we consider the context in which Christiana's dream appears, we become aware of a level of meaning that I deem basic for the understanding of her entire story. The context is as follows: the dream in which Christian appears as a heavenly harpist prompts Christiana's conversion. Shortly after the dream, Christiana is visited by a man who brings her a message from God: God is prepared to forgive her the sin of hard-heartedness, committed against her husband when she refused to comply with his desire for the conversion of the entire family. Christiana, in other words, is tormented by a sense of guilt. It was not Christian who ran away from her; rather, it was she who left him by rejecting his wish for conversion. Indebted to Sigmund Freud's *Interpretation of Dreams*, we may distinguish two sets of content in the dream – one manifest and known, and another one latent and unknown but recoverable through interpretation. What is reported of the dream is its manifest side – Christiana witnesses a heavenly scene that is in keeping with the words of the book of Revelation. The latent content is hinted at by the presence of her husband in the dream, for his presence is the dream's most striking feature. He is at the centre of her mind's preoccupation. The interpretation of a dream is always to be based on its latent content. Obviously, Christiana wants to be reconciled with her husband and to be reunited with him. This desire is repressed by a kind of censorship, as can be seen from the biblical scene that places Christian among the heavenly harpists, presenting him as someone who seeks to worship God rather than seeking the companionship of his wife.

Indebted as it is to Freud, our interpretation may seem inappropriate; yet it finds support from Bunyan's narrative. During her pilgrimage, Christiana is consistently presented as the wife – or widow – of Christian, always introducing herself thus to others.[110] An episode that tells of the family's arrival at a hostelry leaves no doubt as to how Christiana defines her identity. The travellers arrive, Christiana introduces herself as the widow of Christian, and the landlord and

---

109 Bunyan, *The Pilgrim's Progress*, p. 224.
110 Bunyan, *The Pilgrim's Progress*, pp. 270, 301, 314.

landlady indeed remember Christian as a previous guest. Christiana asks to be given the room in which Christian had stayed, a wish easily granted.[111] Of special interest is the ensuing dialogue between Christiana and Mercy:

> *Christiana*: Little did I think once when my husband went on pilgrimage I should ever a [= have] followed.
> *Mercy*: And you as little thought of lying in his bed, and in his chamber to rest as you do now.
> *Christiana*: And much less did I ever think of seeing his face with comfort, and of worshipping the Lord the King with him, and now I believe I shall.[112]

Now you are already in Christian's bed, Mercy says, and Christiana agrees. Soon she will meet Christian, and soon she will worship the Lord together with him! As in our analysis of Christiana's dream, two types of affirmation can be distinguished – one human and one religious. *Humanly* considered, Christiana yearns to be reunited with her husband, and she already rests – though still without him – in his bed. *Religiously* considered, she wishes to pay homage to God as the heavenly king. Both affirmations – the merely human and the religious – intersect in the somewhat unusual expression 'seeing his face with comfort', meaning, approximately, 'seeing his face with pleasure'. The expression is highly ambiguous, for it manages to refer both to seeing God and to seeing the husband. The vocabulary as such is loaded with religious connotation: 'comfort', while generally denoting consolation in situations of distress, may in Bunyan refer to heavenly reward; 'to see God' or 'his face' is a well-known, often-used image that defines what humans desire of heavenly existence. The scriptural basis can be found in the book of Revelation: 'His servants shall serve him; and they shall see his face.'[113] While Christiana uses an expression pregnant with religious meaning, she nevertheless at the moment of speaking seems simply to have her husband in mind. In the language of Freud we can say: without intending to do so, Christiana reveals her actual, non-religious wish – she wants to be with her husband. Although she mentions God, it is to see her husband that she ultimately desires – or at least equally strongly as wishing to see God.

Both levels of this scene are continued in the subsequent narration – the orthodox, ecclesiastical notion of a theocentric heaven, and the human desire for reunion with the beloved.

---

111 Bunyan, *The Pilgrim's Progress*, p. 272.
112 Bunyan, *The Pilgrim's Progress*, 272.
113 Revelation 22:4. As a further biblical passage Psalm 11:7 can be quoted: the righteous may behold the face of God. On visual contact with the deity (not a common notion today) in the Bible, see Bernhard Lang, 'Sehen und Schauen'. In: Manfred Görg et al. (eds.), *Neues Bibel-Lexikon*, Zurich 2001, vol. 3, cols. 555–561.

The ecclesiastical origin of the theocentric viewpoint is made clear in a scene that also takes place in the hostelry mentioned above. Prudence, a teacher who works in the hostel (which somehow doubles as a church), examines the religious knowledge of Christiana's sons, asking them questions from the catechism. The question 'What is heaven?' is answered as follows: 'A place, and state most blessed, because God dwelleth there.'[114] A further question is: 'Why wouldst thou go to Heaven?' Again, the answer is theocentric: 'That I may see God, and serve him without weariness; that I may see Christ, and love him everlastingly; that I may have the fullness of the Holy Spirit in me, that I can by no means here enjoy.'[115] Father, Son, and Holy Spirit are listed here, the complete Trinity. Bunyan seizes every opportunity to affirm his theocentric orthodoxy.[116]

But the other notion of heavenly existence is developed with equal clarity. Christian has provoked all kinds of rumours, and these provide some initial insight:

> The people talk strangely about him. Some say that he now walks in white, that he has a chain of gold about his neck, that he has a crown of gold beset with pearls upon his head. Others say that the Shining Ones that sometimes showed themselves to him on his journey are become his companions, and that he is familiar with them in the place where he is as here one neighbour is with another. Besides, 'tis confidently affirmed concerning him, that the King of the place where he is, has bestowed upon him already a very rich and pleasant dwelling at court, and that he every day eateth and drinketh, and walketh, and talketh with him, and receiveth the smiles and favours of him that is Judge of all there.[117]

The reader immediately senses that Bunyan is aiming here at something different. The theocentric perspective is still somehow present, but the lofty God of heaven is transformed into a friendly lord and master whose domestic, more than courtly, life Christian shares and enjoys. There is no mention of praise and liturgical worship; the liturgical relationship of service is replaced by a sense of easy familiarity that makes us forget that Bunyan was actually speaking about a human being and his creator and judge. Now Christian is the central figure, and we might almost conclude that God himself has become the servant. In fact, Bunyan goes on to explain just this: soon, the judge will visit our country to find

---

114 Bunyan, *The Pilgrim's Progress*, p. 276.
115 Bunyan, *The Pilgrim's Progress*, p. 276.
116 The theocentric view is expressed quite clearly in Bunyan's own catechism *Instruction for the Ignorant* (1675) where he exhorts the reader: 'Be often remembering what a blessed thing it is to be saved, to go to Heaven, to be made like angels, and to dwell with God and Christ to all eternity.' John Bunyan, *Instruction for the Ignorant – Light for Them that Sit in Darkness – Saved by Grace – Come, & Welcome, to Jesus Christ*. Edited by Richard L. Greaves, Oxford 1979, p. 44.
117 Bunyan, *The Pilgrim's Progress*, p. 221.

out why Christian, his friend, was treated so badly by the people, for whatever they have done to Christian, he will consider a personal insult – 'he will look upon all as if done unto himself'.[118] All of a sudden we see Christian placed at the centre, and we are justified in speaking of an anthropocentric notion.

Whereas in the anthropocentric rumour about Christian's heavenly existence Christiana remains unmentioned, this is no longer the case with another passage. Bunyan presents a dialogue between two travellers: Great-heart (the well-known protector and travel companion of Christiana and her children) and Valiant-for-Truth, a pilgrim who chances upon our group. As the two are talking, the subject of Christian comes up. Valiant-for-Truth has heard of his adventures, and to his surprise now learns that Christiana, too, has taken to the road for the heavenly city. Here is part of the dialogue:

> *Valiant-for Truth*: Why, is this Christian's wife?
> *Great-heart*: Yes, that it is, and these are also her four sons.
> *Valiant-for-Truth*: What! And going on pilgrimage too?
> *Great-heart*: Yes, verily, they are following after.
> *Valiant-for-Truth*: It glads me at the heart! Good man! How joyful will he be when he shall see them that would not go with him, yet to enter after him in at the Gates into the City?
> *Great-heart*: Without doubt it will be a comfort to him; for next to the joy of seeing himself there, it will be a joy to meet there his wife and his children.
> *Valiant-for-Truth*: But now you are upon that, pray let me see your opinion about it. Some make a question whether we shall know one another when we are there.
> *Great-heart*: Do they think they know themselves then? Or that they shall rejoice to see themselves in that bliss? And if they think they shall know and do these; why not know others, and rejoice in their welfare also? – Again, since relations are our second self, though that state will be dissolved there, yet why may it not be rationally concluded that we shall be more glad to see them there than to see they are wanting?
> *Valiant-for-Truth*: Well, I perceive whereabouts you are as to this.[119]

Like all of Bunyan's dialogues, this one begins as a fast exchange. The stranger comes out with a very natural remark: Christian will be happy about the arrival of his wife and children. Great-heart agrees and does not mind being questioned further by the stranger: well, there is this theological controversy about recognising others in heaven – which, according to some, is impossible. At this point Bunyan gives his Great-heart the role of a theological expert who sketches a theology based not on biblical evidence but exclusively on rational arguments. If it is true that individuals will not lose their own identity (implying memory of the past life on earth), then one has also to assume that they will remember other individuals. Accordingly, each of the blessed will not only rejoice in his or her own bliss, but also in the bliss of others known to him or her. Here we no longer

---

118 Bunyan, *The Pilgrim's Progress*, p. 221.
119 Bunyan, *The Pilgrim's Progress*, p. 351

listen to Bunyan the poet but to Bunyan the theological thinker, and the line of thought is to his credit.

One feature of this dialogue merits being underlined: there is no reference to God; the discussion is about human bliss, and nothing else. The theocentric line of thought remains unmentioned, the anthropocentric argument alone being highlighted. Heaven, we must conclude, may also be considered from a merely human perspective.

This is all Bunyan tells us about heaven. We are already near the end of the story. The pilgrims approach the heavenly city from which they remain separated by the river of death. Christiana blesses her children, and then dies, in order to proceed to the heavenly gate. Her children stay behind, apparently joining the community of believers where they settle down.

At this point we may return to the question posed at the beginning: how shall we define the theological position of Bunyan? Is he opting for a theocentric heaven as does Baxter, who never misses an opportunity to assert it? Or is he opting for an anthropocentric hereafter, more in keeping with the mind of Milton? Generally speaking, volume one of *The Pilgrim's Progress* is dominated by a theocentric image of heaven, whereas volume two leans towards the anthropocentric model without, however, completely replacing theocentricsm. Both ideas coexist in juxtaposition, but how they might relate to each other is not discussed.

However, this way of looking at things is not entirely satisfactory. I have the impression that Bunyan actually wanted to portray the human side of heaven, but did not dare confide his developing thoughts to his book. At the end of his second volume, Bunyan takes leave of his readers with a final 'Adieu', but also leaves them much food for thought. By not actually giving the story a proper ending, he invites his readers to imagine a conclusion. But the readers are not completely left on their own, for Bunyan has done much to feed their imagination – with intimations and sketches of anthropocentric celestial existence. As early as the first volume he refers to heavenly reunion, almost as an aside: 'There you shall enjoy your friends again', confidently state the Shining Ones, i.e. the angels.[120] In the second volume, the anthropocentric imagination gains in clarity and detail, and is no longer heard from the angels but from human beings. Only once does Christiana herself express the relevant ideas. At the very beginning of the Christiana narrative it is a Mr. Sagacity who reports on the rumours of Christian's heavenly life; recipient of this report is the meta-narrator, i.e. Bunyan himself. Then it is Mercy, rather than Christiana, who refers to Christiana's wish to rest in her husband's bed at the hostel. Later, Valiant-for-

---

120 Bunyan, *The Pilgrim's Progress*, p. 201.

Truth and Great-heart discuss heavenly reunion, whereby the stranger – Valiant-for-Truth – brings up the subject, while Great-heart, for a moment abandoning his role of the knightly protector, plays the theologian. We can sense that the author, conscious of the problem, has placed great restraint on Christiana. Nevertheless, we understand Christiana's desire for her lost husband as the hidden and maybe unconscious motive for her pilgrimage.

William Blake

This could very well be the end of the present essay. However, I have found an eminent interpreter of the work of Bunyan who provides a conclusion to *The Pilgrim's Progress* that is both original and convincing. Living more than a hundred years after Bunyan in the same country, he ranks as one of England's most celebrated poets. I am speaking of William Blake (1757–1827). The narrative medium he used is not textual but visual. Among the papers left by Blake, an incomplete and unfinished cycle of illustrations for *The Pilgrim's Progress* was found.[121] This cycle is just one example of Blake's interest in illustrating the great works of world literature: the Bible, Vergil, Dante, and Milton. There are 33 illustrations, all of scenes from part one of *The Pilgrim's Progress*. Blake specialists date the cycle to 1824 to 1827, but an earlier etching exists, also depicting a scene from part one, dated to 1794.[122] For more than three decades, or so it seems, Blake took an interest in Bunyan, apparently without being commissioned. I claim to have discovered one more of Blake's illustrations for *The Pilgrim's Progress*: an etching until now not fully understood, depicting, I contend, a scene from the second part of the novel – the heavenly reunion of Christian and Christiana.

The etching (Fig. 3.1) can be found in an illustrated edition of a long poem published in 1808: Robert Blair's *The Grave*.[123] Written in 1743, this blend of awe-inspiring cemetery poetry and religious confession still had a readership in

---

121 Martin Butlin, *The Paintings and Drawings of William Blake*. Text, New Haven 1981, pp. 599–606 (catalogue nos. 829–834); on this cycle, see Gerda S. Norvig, *Dark Figures in the Desired Country: Blake's Illustrations to The Pilgrim's Progress*, Berkeley 1993.
122 Illustration in Norvig, *Dark Figures in the Desired Country*, p. 52. For the dating, see Geoffrey Keynes, *Blake Studies. Essays on His Life and Work*. 2nd ed., Oxford 1971, p. 165; Norvig, *Dark Figures in the Desired Country*, p. 284 n. 2. The scene depicted – 'The Man Sweeping the Interpreter's Parlour' – can be found in Bunyan, *The Pilgrim's Progress*, p. 61.
123 Robert Blair, *The Grave. Illustrated by William Blake*. A Study with Facsimile by Robert N. Essick and Morton D. Paley, London 1982; the illustration is between p. 8 and p. 9.

Figure 3.1: William Blake, The Meeting of a Family in Heaven. – The two angels who frame the scene indicate its heavenly setting. Blake's original sketch most likely belongs to a series of illustrations he planned for the Pilgrim's Progress. At the end of this novel, members of the family who travel separately to the celestial city are reunited in paradise.

the early nineteenth century. The illustrations are by Blake, the engraving being done by Louis Schiavonetti. The print of interest here is entitled 'The Meeting of a Family in Heaven', though this theme is completely absent from Blair's poem, and the question is: how did this illustration get into the book?

To find an answer, we must prepare ourselves by considering the fact that Blake, when doing commissioned work, often borrowed from his earlier work. Blake, the modern editors of *The Grave* tell us, 'completed the twenty or so *Grave* designs in a very short time, probably less than two months. It was always his practice to rummage his earlier works for images to use in current projects, but the pressure of time seems to have forced more borrowings than usual'.[124] The borrowings are from works made in the 1780s and 1790s. In the light of this consideration, the following conjecture seems plausible: put to secondary use by Blake, 'The Meeting of a Family in Heaven' originated in a different context, and this context can be identified as Blake's early, 1790s work on Bunyan illustrations. According to part two of *The Pilgrim's Progress*, it will be joyful for Christian '*to meet there* [in heaven] *his wife and his children*'. The very wording of the title – 'the meeting' – echoes the text of Bunyan. What Blake was seeking to portray, therefore, is how Christian met his wife and his children. If we follow the events as told in *The Pilgrim's Progress*, this cannot be right after Christiana's death, for the children stay alive on earth; only much later, after the death of all of them, will they enter the celestial city in order to be united with their parents – with Christian and Christiana. Blake placed Christian and Christiana at the centre. Framed by a pair of angels, they embrace tightly, while the tips of the angelic wings meet to form a gothic arch. Later, Blake was to sketch a similar scene in the Bunyan cycle; in it Christian and Hopeful, accompanied by two angels with wings outspread, enter the heavenly city (Fig. 3.2).[125] In Blake's 'Meeting of a Family in Heaven' we can discern three of the four sons of the celestial pair. On the right, one of the sons approaches the parents with arms outstretched, ready to embrace them. To the left and to the right we can discern – kneeling and standing, respectively – two more couples shown as they embrace. Blake's rendering is based on a close reading of Bunyan's text: the sons of Christiana and Christian are already married, and it would detract from the idyllic atmosphere if the daughters-in-law were excluded from the heavenly scene. The five children depicted by Blake can be identified as three sons and two daughters-in-law. A more complete rendering, with four

---

124 Essick and Paley, 'Commentary on the Designs', in: Blair, *The Grave*, pp. 45–54, here p. 52.
125 Butlin, *The Paintings and Drawings of William Blake*. Text, p. 605 (catalogue no. 829 – 29). A good reproduction in colour can be found in Norvig, *Dark Figures in the Desired Country*, plate 28.

Figure 3.2: William Blake, Christian and Hopeful at the Gate of Heaven. – This illustration of a scene from the Pilgrim's Progress includes features reminiscent of the etching 'The Meeting of a Family in Heaven' (Fig. 4.1).

sons and their spouses, would have meant a crowded picture that would lack the emblematic character intended by the artist. Blake, in other words, gives us a selection of family members that nevertheless, serving *as pars pro toto*, indicates completeness. We can also find an answer to the question why the sons and their spouses are depicted as children rather than as adults: exclusively filled with adults, the picture would no longer be immediately suggestive of 'The Meeting of a Family in Heaven'.

The Pilgrim's Progress, we must add, accounts only in part for the motif depicted by Blake. If we dig deeper into Blake's intellectual world, we cannot pass by Emanuel Swedenborg, the visionary who died in London in 1772. Blake, fascinated with Swedenborg's celestial visions, was a member of London's Swedenborgian community.[126] He studied Swedenborg's *Heaven and Hell*, a book which, departing from Christian tradition, teaches the continuation of the marriage bond in the hereafter. Whereas in Christian tradition marriage ends at death and is not renewed in heaven, Swedenborg cannot think of heavenly existence without the close companionship of husband and wife. Blake, upon discovering this notion in Bunyan, did not hesitate to give it pictorial expression.

It is to Blake, then, that we owe the real conclusion to *The Pilgrim's Progress*, the scene of heavenly reunion missing from Bunyan's novel. Bunyan himself, while hinting at the matter, apparently did not dare to be more explicit, for this would have led him too far away from theocentric orthodoxy. Free from such a scrupulous attitude, the artist portrayed Christian and Christiana and their children as they meet in heaven. That the artist has not completely misunderstood the religious thinker can be seen from the following lines of Bunyan:

> Our friends that lived godly here,
> Shall there be found again;
> The wife, the child, and father dear,
> With others of our train.[127]

Blake does not create anything new. Nor does he add anything to Bunyan. He merely explains, completes, and brings to a satisfactory conclusion.

---

126 G.E. Bentley, *Blake Records*, Oxford 1969, pp. 34–38; Peter Ackroyd, *William Blake. Dichter, Maler, Visionär*, Munich 1995, pp. 111–115.
127 John Bunyan, 'One Thing Is Needful; or, Serious Meditations upon the Four Last Things' [1665], in: John Bunyan, *The Poems*. Edited by Graham Midgley, Oxford 1980, p. 88.

Summary

The Pilgrim's Progress (1676, 1684), a two-part novel of religious instruction and edification by the English Puritan John Bunyan, depicts the life of the believer who, in preparation for everlasting bliss, turns away from a world marked by the darkness of vice and sin. Like other writings of this author, this work includes several brief passages from which we learn how Bunyan feels about life everlasting. Beyond the heavenly gate the blessed join the heavenly hosts. Assimilated to the angelic hosts, they may sing and play their harps to the praise of God in all eternity. This strictly theocentric view vies with, and is mitigated by, another version of celestial existence. The alternative view, anthropocentric in nature, emerges with increasing clarity in the second part of the novel: in eternal life, believing families and married couples are reunited. For Christiana, heroine of the novel's second volume, the desire to be reunited with her deceased husband, now resident in heaven, is the (albeit hidden) motive to leave the City of Destruction and take to the road as a pilgrim. An etching published in 1808, based on a drawing by William Blake, carries the legend: 'The Meeting of a Family in Heaven'. With its three embracing couples presumably inspired by a passage of *The Pilgrim's Progress*, it provides Bunyan's novel with a conclusion barely hinted at by the novelist: at the end, we will all be meeting again in heaven.

Postscript

Until recently, Blake's 'Meeting of a Family in Heaven' was known only through Louis Schiavonetti's engraving (fig. 3.1). In 2001, a book dealer from Yorkshire stumbled across a calfskin portfolio in an antiquarian shop in Glasgow. The maroon case contained nineteen watercolours by Blake, including the 'Meeting of a Family in Heaven'. The individual items were subsequently sold to anonymous buyers by Sotheby's, so that their present locations are unknown. Luckily however, the entire lot was photographed, and a facsimile published: Martin Butlin (ed.), *William Blake's Watercolour Inventions in Illustration of* The Grave *by Robert Blair*, Lavenham, Suffolk: The William Blake Trust 2009.

Chapter 4: The Spanish Heaven. Opposition to Modernity

In an interview published in 1969, the Spanish essayist Elisa Lamas explains that she is hoping for the continuation of human love in the other world. Considering the question of whether death could mean the final separation from her husband and her seven sons, she declares: 'I do not understand how someone could live a life of shared love when he or she is convinced that each day that passes means a day less with the beloved, and that one day the sun must rise over the final parting. I do not understand how parents could confront the death of a child when they expect never to see it again.'[128]

Similar sentiments are expressed in epitaphs found in cemeteries: death means separation from the loved person, but there will be reunion in the other life. Two examples from the cemetery of Salamanca show how the idea is typically expressed: 'O good Jesus, deign that they might not be eternally separated from those whom they have loved so much on earth', reads a 1981 gravestone inscription that takes the form of a prayer. Another, from 1969, signs a votive plaque, 'Your parents and brothers – until heaven'.[129] While such sentiments appeal to our sensibilities and sound natural, they do not seem to have made much impact on the theology and literature of Catholic Spain. This can be seen most clearly in baroque theology that is generally prepared to grant the saints some form of a social life. In a sermon delivered at the beatification of Teresa of Avila in 1614, the royal preacher Jerónimo da Florencia (1565–1633) waxed eloquent when it came to describing the nun's reception into the celestial court: her reception was grander, he asserted, than anyone else's but the Virgin Mary, and upon her arrival, she was eagerly sought by all angels and saints.[130] Somewhat more detail can be culled from the work of Martín de Roa (1561–1637), one of Jerónimo's fellow Jesuits. Martín describes the social world of heaven in the context of a chapter dedicated to the qualities that the glorified

---

128 José Maria Gironella, *100 Españoles y Dios*, Madrid 1969, p. 309.
129 'Dignaos ¡o! Buen Jesús no separen la eternidad a los que tanto se amaron en la tierra.' – 'Tus padres y hermanos hasta el cielo.' Collected in 1983.
130 Jerónimo de Florencia, quoted in Carlos M.N. Eire, *From Madrid to Purgatory: The Art and Craft of Dying in Sixteenth-Century Spain*, Cambridge: Cambridge University Press, 1995, p. 523 n. 43.

bodies of the blessed will have in the next world.[131] Not only does perfect health belong to the glorified body, but also a renewed sense of touch, he asserts. Thus the blessed will enjoy kissing the hands and feet of Christ and his mother, and derive much pleasure from touching the glorified bodies of their fellow saints. Fathers, sons and friends in particular will travel to the place of the beloved, where they will be welcomed with holy kisses. Holding each other in holy embrace, they will exchange compliments, and holding hands, they will converse, discussing the sublime ways by which divine providence has brought them to the world of everlasting joy. While Father Martín imagines these touching scenes of reunion, he seems to impose restrictions on his imagination. He studiously avoids going into more detail, and especially, discussing any male-female relationships in the other world. The existence of social life among the blessed is not denied, but even in baroque literature its description remains vague.

Catholic authors and artists have not taken much note of Elisa Lamas's family-centred heaven or Father Martín de Roa's heaven of friendly discourse; instead, they portray a heaven in which the blessed focus so enthusiastically and exclusively on the divine centre that every thought of other creatures vanishes. This theocentric notion of the hereafter can be documented from all periods of Spanish history, from the early Middle Ages to the contemporary period.

One particularly graphic example comes from Pedro de Medina (1493–1567), otherwise known as royal cosmographer and author of a manual of navigation. In his *Libro de la Verdad* (Book of Truth, 1555) he offers a portrait of the celestial court.[132] As if in a showcase, the blessed are spatially arranged in a rigid hierarchy where everyone has his or her proper station for eternity. At the very summit of the court, the Triune God reigns as the supreme monarch. Below the trinity, the Virgin Mary reigns as queen of heaven, gloriously clad in superb apparel, 'according to the dignity and worthiness that belong to such a high lady'. Below Mary, the angelic hosts are arrayed like an army or government officials, and given names such as knights, royal officials, and supervisors of the treasury. Below the angels, the saints, too, are eternally arranged according to their merit. There is no hint of the blessed interacting among themselves or with saints and angels. What we are given is an image of rigid order and immobility, with God at the top. All the residents of heaven seem to share this divine immutability. Pedro de Medina's description echoes how artists sought to

---

131 Martín de Roa, *Estado de los Bienaventurados en el Cielo*, Barcelona 1630, fol. 49, as quoted in a study of heaven and hell in seventeenth-century Spain: Ana Martínez Arancón, *Geografía de la eternidad*, Madrid 1987, p. 262.
132 Eire, *From Madrid to Purgatory*, p. 523.

visualise the feast of 'all saints'; celebrated on the first of November, it opposes the fading, transient realm of nature with the eternal stability and splendour of the celestial world. When we ask what the blessed actually do in heaven, we have to turn elsewhere, for Pedro de Medina has no answer. One response can be found for instance in *Las cortes de la muerte* (The courts of death), a religious play by the playwright Lope de Vega (1562–1635). He has an angel explain that 'God lives eternally within walls of sapphire that are speckled with topaz. In his palace the Thrones and the Powers shout forever their cry "holy, holy", while the blessed spirits in their glory see and love that undivided Essence, of which each attribute radiates immeasurable splendour'.[133] This is a heaven of angels (with their traditional subcategories 'Thrones' and 'Powers'), the Trinity (in scholastic language, the 'undivided Essence'), and the blessed ones who eagerly contemplate and study the divine attributes. Lope de Vega no doubt echoes here the theological training he received from the Jesuits.

Theological textbooks published in the late twentieth century offer a portrait of heaven that is as theocentric (or Christocentric) as is the heaven of Pedro de Medina and Lope de Vega. According to the Jesuit Cándido Pozo, author of the most widely used textbook on the 'theology of the beyond', heaven means 'closeness to God',[134] and nothing else; not a word is wasted on the discussion of heavenly reunion and the social life of the saints. José Grau, a Protestant author writing in 1980, presents heaven in no less theocentric terms: 'Heaven is heaven', he states in the book's concluding sentence, 'because of the Lord's presence, and even hell would be heaven if Christ could be found there'.[135] Accordingly, it does not come as a surprise to find the following definition in an encyclopaedia of general knowledge: heaven is 'the mansion in which the angels, the saints and the blessed enjoy the presence of God'.[136] A little, but only a little, more descriptive is José María Escrivá de Balaguer (1902–1975), priest and founder of the conservative Catholic movement 'Opus Dei'. In a sermon he explains that 'heaven is the purpose of our worldly way. Jesus Christ went ahead. He waits there for us himself, together with the Mother of God, Saint Joseph [...] the angels, and the saints.'[137] Although this heaven is peopled here with saints and angels, Escrivá is far from indulging in the sentimental speculations of an Elisa Lamas.

---

133 Lope de Vega, *Obras*, vol. 8 (Biblioteca de autores españoles 159), Madrid 1963, p. 471.
134 Cándido Pozo, *Teología del más allá*, 3rd ed., Madrid 1992, p. 406: 'intimidad con Dios'.
135 José Grau, *Escatología: las últimas cosas* (Curso de la formación teológica evangélica 7), Terrassa 1980, p. 427.
136 *Diccionario Enciclopedico Espasa*. 8th ed., Madrid 1978, vol. 4, p. 3.
137 José María Escrivá, *Amigos de Dios*, Madrid 1977, p. 322.

For most Spanish Christians, then, heavenly life has little connection with earthly life: human needs, wishes, feelings, and emotions have no place in a heaven where God is the focus of all attention. In what follows I offer a tentative analysis and explanation of this puzzling fact. I will point out several factors that seem to have contributed to the shaping of the Spanish notion of heaven. The first factor, surprisingly, is the strong influence of Islam in medieval Spain.

The Islamic factor

The Muslim conquerors of Spain brought with them a heaven oriented toward human enjoyment and not toward eternal praise. The heaven depicted in the Qu'ran, the sacred book of all Muslims, is reserved for the righteous who believe in God and do his good works.[138] Eternal bliss occurs not immediately after death but at the end of time, when the good go to live in the coolness of paradise and the evil go to a fiery hell. Only the souls of martyrs enter heaven immediately. The Islamic heaven is a garden (*janna*), endowed with temperate climate, shade-giving trees, peaceful and secure. They drink delicious wine from a stream and never feel any untoward after-effects (Sura 37:45–47). Men enjoy the company of the *hûr*: beautiful virgins created specifically for the male residents of paradise. Although the Qu'ran is silent on the subject, later tradition explains that men will be even more sexually active with the Hur than they were with earthy women, and that the Hur can even produce offspring if the man so wishes. On earth, virtuous women (*mu'minat*) have only one husband. It is unclear whom they will meet in paradise if they have several mates on earth. Women's life in heaven, while assumed, is not described.

The human-oriented heaven of the Qu'ran is only part of the traditional Islamic understanding of eternal life. While mentioned only briefly in the Qu'ran, the prophet Muhammad's nightly ascension (*mi'râj*) from Jerusalem to the throne of God also provides hints for understanding what happens to the righteous soul after the resurrection. Elaborations of the otherworldly journeys of Muhammad are contained in the Hadith, the post-Qur'anic body of traditions relating to the life of the prophet.[139] According to these traditions, the prophet's

---

138 For the Islamic concept of heaven I rely on Jane Idleman Smith and Yvonne Yazbeck Haddad, *The Islamic Understanding of Death and Resurrection*, Oxford 2002. On the Hur, see pp. 164–168.

139 An important Arabic source, the *Kiâb al-mi'râj* (Book of the Ascension), survives only in a Latin translation that circulated among medieval Christians. For a German translation and discussion of this source, see Edeltraud Werner, *Die Jenseitsreise Mohammeds – Liber Scale Machometi*, Hildesheim 2007.

ascent to the throne of God first took him to a garden where he met his friends and the prophets Abraham, Moses, and Jesus. The journey concluded at the throne of God where Muhammad beheld seventy rows of angels chanting unending hymns of praise. Everything was bathed in a sea of light. Such divine radiance at first filled Muhammad with fear, but soon his misgivings were dispelled and a sense of spiritual insight came over him. The divine presence entirely eclipsed the more human-oriented paradise garden. 'And as I gazed upon it', one legend has the prophet reflect, 'all the works of creation sank into insignificance. The seven heavens, the seven earths, the seven hells, [...] the whole of creation compared to that throne, was like a tiny ring of the mesh of a coat of mail lying in the midst of a boundless desert.'[140]

Ibn Arabi of Murcia (d. 1240), the Spanish Muslim philosopher and mystic, understood Muhammad's spiritual journey to mean that heaven was far more than merely a place to gratify human desires. Those who could only perceive heaven as a place for refined earthly joys were of a lower spiritual development than those who participated in the divine glory. 'There are two heavens,' he wrote, 'the one, sensible; and the other, ideal. In the one, both the animal and the rational souls enjoy bliss; in the other, the rational souls alone. The latter paradise is the heaven of knowledge and intuition.'[141] The Islamic perception of heaven, like the Christian, includes images of a strongly God-oriented heaven. Both traditions draw upon a Neoplatonic repertoire of themes by invoking ascension, spiritual refinement, and eventual participation in the fullness of God. The focal point of eternal life is not human enjoyment but divine praise.

Perhaps the theocentric Islamic heaven helped shape the medieval Christian heaven as the Spanish scholar and priest Miguel Asín Palacios (1871–1944) believed. Asín Palacios argued that Dante's inspiration for the Divine Comedy had its source in Islamic beliefs and traditions, and more recent scholarship, while being more nuanced than Asín, actually supports this interpretation.[142] But while Christian and Islamic authors agreed on the theocentric side of heaven, the anthropocentric side, dear as it was to Islamic tradition, prompted controversy. In their apologetics, Christian theologians came to disagree strongly with a sensuous concept of paradise. One of them was Raimundus Lullus (1235–1315).

---

140 Miguel Asín Palacios, *Islam and the Divine Comedy*. Translated by Harold Sunderland, New York 1926, p. 22. Asín Palacios attributes this passage to one of the two eighth-century writers: a Persian, Maysara son of Abd ar-Rabihi, or Omar son of Sulayman, who lived in Damascus.
141 Ibn Arabi, as quoted in Asín Palacios, *Islam and the Divine Comedy*, p. 138.
142 Philip F. Kennedy, 'Muslim Sources of Dante?', in: Dionysius A. Agius and Richard Hitchcock (eds.), *The Arab Influence in Medieval Europe*, Reading 1994, pp. 63–82; Giuseppe Tardiola, "Ancor nel libro suo che Scala ha nome ..." *Letteratura Italiana Antica* 1 (2000): 59–67; Werner, *Die Jenseitsreise Mohammeds*, pp. 19–20.

Lull, as he is called in Spanish, was born and grew up on the island of Mallorca which at that time had a substantial Muslim population. He wrote in Latin, Catalan, and Arabic, and his missionary travels took him to North Africa, Cyprus, Armenia, and Jerusalem. Lull believed that all articles of the Christian faith could be proven philosophically. Philosophy and theology ultimately were one. In his *Book on the Gentile and the Three Sages* (late 1270s) Lull stets forth a dialogue in which three sages, a Jew, a Muslim and a Christian, tell a Gentile about the essence of each of their religions.[143] The book became popular and was translated from Catalan into Latin, French, Arabic, and Hebrew. Lull's Muslim sage explains that in paradise people will have both spiritual and bodily glory. Spiritual glory implies the vision of God and the love of him. Bodily glory consists in the delights of the senses. In heaven there will be palaces with magnificent rooms, and for men, access to beautiful virgins. Lull explains through the mouthpiece of the Muslim sage that men will enjoy sexual relations with these women who, despite their compliance, retain their youth and virginity for ever.

For the Christian, however, there will be no such life. Lull has the Christian sage describe a thoroughly theocentric heaven where there will be no eating, drinking, or readily available women. The hardships and iniquities of this life will not be rewarded with sensual joys but rather with seeing and listening to the Trinity. In heaven the righteous will observe the relationship between the Father, Son, the Holy Spirit, and the Virgin Mary. They will see how the ranks of the angels, archangels, martyrs, virgins, confessors, and all the saints unite in sweet songs of praise and glory. The Christian heaven, in contrast with the Islamic heaven, consists of the beatific vision and eternal praise of the divine. At the end of the book, Lull has the Christian sage affirm that the Christian view is superior to that of the Muslims or Jews because it is more in tune with basic philosophical concepts. The Christian heaven, for Lull, is more rational because it allows for the participation in divine glory and not in activities typical of human beings.

Was there Muslim influence on Spanish concepts of heaven? The answer must be: yes and no. While the theocentric mysticism of Ibn Arabi might have found acceptance, the human-oriented heaven of the Qu'ran was firmly rejected. Theocentric teachings received support from those who rejected specifically Islamic notions of life in post-mortem paradise. They received even more support from Christian mystics.

---

143 Ramón Llull, *Obres essencials*, Barcelona 1957, vol. 1, pp. 1131–1133 (Islamic paradise), 1104–1105 (Christian paradise).

Spanish mysticism

Through the writings of three sixteenth-century religious thinkers and saints – Teresa of Avila, John of the Cross, and Luis de León – we can explore the connection between the soul's experience of the divine through meditation and the fuller perception of God after death in heaven. Teresa of Avila (1515–1582) and John of the Cross (1542–1591), the great mystics, wrote only sporadically about what good Christians would encounter after death. Their major concern was to describe a spiritual path that would, in this life, allow the soul to fully encounter God. Through the process of purgation, illumination, and eventual unity with the divine, the soul would achieve a taste of what awaits it in heaven. Before the spiritual marriage of the soul with Christ, Teresa explains in the *Interior Castle* (1577), the soul is brought to the seventh room, to provide a dwelling place for the Lord. 'For just as in heaven', she writes, 'so in the soul His Majesty must have a room where He dwells alone. Let us call it another heaven.'[144] At its highest level, contemplation permits the anticipation of face-to-face vision of God after death. For the mystic, it is not important to see heaven in vision but rather to experience God in the depths of meditation.

If the depths of meditation allow anticipation of heaven, what is the character of that heaven? For Teresa, when the soul is brought to the dwelling place of the Lord 'the most blessed Trinity, all three persons, through an intellectual vision, is revealed to it through a certain representation of the truth'.[145] The soul experiences a glimpse of the beatific vision and is permitted to understand the mystery of the relationship between Father, Son, and Holy Spirit. Heaven – as anticipated on earth – is made up of the vision and knowledge of the divine mystery. Seeing and understanding, however, are accompanied by a more profound intimacy. The soul who is given a taste of 'the glory of heaven' also is 'made one with God'.[146] In the centre of the soul, as in heaven, a spiritual marriage takes place. The soul is united with God, 'like the bright light entering a room through two different windows: although the streams of light are separate when entering the room, they become one'.[147] The essence of heaven is the unification of the soul with the divine.

The unity of the soul with God in eternal life was recognised by John of the Cross as the transformation of the soul into the divine. In eternal life, the soul

---

144 Teresa of Avila, *The Interior Castle* VII, 1,3 (Teresa of Avila, *The Interior Castle*. Translated by Kiernan Kavanaugh and Otilio Rodriguez, New York 1979, p. 173).
145 Teresa of Avila, *The Interior Castle* VII, 1,6 (p. 175).
146 Teresa of Avila, *The Interior Castle* VII, 2,3 (p. 178).
147 Teresa of Avila, *The Interior Castle* VII, 2,4 (p. 179).

reflects the beauty of God and God sees his own beauty in the soul. *The Spiritual Canticle* (1584) presents this as a tautology: 'Both of us are in your beauty alone, I (the soul) being absorbed in your (God's) beauty; hence, I shall see you in your beauty, and you shall see me in your beauty, and I shall see myself in you in your beauty, and you will see yourself in me in your beauty.'[148] God becomes the soul and the soul participates and shares in the nature of the divine. For John of the Cross, this unity of God and soul is so thorough that in eternal life, the human soul becomes divine. '[Human] souls possess the same blessings by participation as He possesses by nature,' John writes, 'for this reason they [human souls] are truly gods by participation, equals of God and His companions.'[149] When this union happens the soul participates 'in God Himself, and it will be performing in Him, in company with Him, the work of the Most Holy Trinity.'[150] In exquisite prose, John uses bridal imagery to portray the deification of the soul:

> The weight of glory to which You predestined me, O my Spouse, on the day of Your eternity, when You considered it good to decree my creation: that glory You will give me there on the day of my betrothal and marriage, on the day of the joy of my heart, when, released from the flesh, admitted into the lofty caverns of Your bridal chamber, and gloriously transformed into You, You shall drink with me the juice of the sweet pomegranates.[151]

Both Teresa and John temper their descriptions of heaven with disclaimers that heavenly glory can only be understood partially. After having been taken up to heaven, Teresa reports that she wanted to describe 'at least some small part of what I learnt, but when I consider how to do so I find it is impossible. The mere difference between the light we see here and the light of vision is inexpressible.[152] In the *Spiritual Canticle* John of the Cross retreats even more vigorously from describing heaven. After citing biblical references describing the bliss of heaven he concluded that 'for a thing of such immensity has the property that all excellent terms that are of quality and greatness and good agree with it, but none of these describes it – nay, nor all of them together.'[153] For the

---

148   John of the Cross, *The Spiritual Canticle* [second redaction], commentary on stanza 36, 5 (John of the Cross, *Selected Writings*. Edited by Kieran Kavanaugh, London 1987, pp. 274–275).
149   John of the Cross, *The Spiritual Canticle* [second redaction], commentary on stanza 39, 6 (*The Complete Works of Saint John of the Cross*. Translated by E. Allison Peers, Wheathampstead 1964, vol. 2, p. 367, modified).
150   John of the Cross, *The Spiritual Canticle*, commentary on stanza 39, 6 (*The Complete Works of Saint John of the Cross*, vol. 2, p. 367).
151   John of the Cross, *The Spiritual Canticle*, commentary on stanza 38, 9 (*The Complete Works of Saint John of the Cross*, vol. 2, p. 373, modified).
152   Teresa, *The Life* 38, 2 (*The Life of Saint Teresa*. Translated by J.M. Cohen, Harmondsworth 1957, p. 284).
153   John of the Cross, *The Spiritual Canticle*, commentary on stanza 38, 8 (*The Complete Works of Saint John of the Cross*, vol. 2, p. 373).

mystic, both limits of language and of understanding preclude any meaningful portrayal of heaven. Only through the spiritual works such as the *Interior Castle* and the *Spiritual Canticle* can one begin to sense the glory of the beatific vision. What is quite clear from these accounts is that heaven implies both the vision and the knowledge of God. From the mystic's perspective, the soul longs for unity with the beloved; for unity with, and transformation into, the divine. Any other concern – the meeting of pre-deceased family members, conversations with the saints, enjoying the pleasures of a paradise garden – has no place in eternity. In Teresa's vision of heaven recounted in her autobiography, she recalls that 'the first persons I saw there were my father and my mother.'[154] She only includes this brief statement and never elaborates on this meeting. For Teresa, meeting one's parents, while perhaps a part of heaven, is in no way a central event. Union with Christ is the ultimate and all-consuming purpose of eternity. 'In this interior union', explains John of the Cross, 'God communicates himself to the soul with such genuine love that no mother's affection, in which she tenderly caresses her child, nor brother's love, nor friendship is comparable to it.'[155] In the heaven of the mystics familial love and friendship are totally eclipsed by the divine. In the words of Teresa of Avila, '*solo Dios basta*' – God alone suffices.[156]

Fray Luis de León (1527?–1591), more influenced by Humanist and Renaissance perspectives on literature and learning than Teresa of Avila and John of the Cross, departs only tentatively from theocentric images of heaven. For Fray Luis, heaven has both the elements of the scholastic empyrean heaven and the classical Elysian Fields. In *To Felipe Ruiz*, Fray Luis wonders when he will fly to heaven from the dungeon where he is imprisoned. In heaven, the poet tells us, he will 'observe the truth pure and unveiled (*contemplar la verdad pura sin velo*).'[157] Following Thomas Aquinas, heaven is the vision of God, luminosity, and endless knowledge:

Converted into light
and shining everywhere, there I will see
my own life, and the sight
of what is joined yet free,
what is and was and its own mystery.[158]

---

154 Teresa, *The Life* 38,1 (*The Life of Saint Teresa*, p. 283).
155 John of the Cross, *The Spiritual Canticle*, introduction to the commentary on stanza 27 (*Selected Writings*, p. 265).
156 A line in Teresa of Avila's famous poem *Nada te turbe*.
157 Luis de León, *To Felipe Ruiz*, Strophe 1 (Luis de León, *The Unknown Light*. Translated by Willis Barnstone, Albany 1979, p. 71).
158 Luis de León, *To Felipe Ruiz*, str. 2 (Luis de León, *The Unknown Light*, p. 71).

In heaven the poet expects to see happy spirits:

> I'll see the dwelling place
> of ecstasy, of joy in a still sphere
> looming in highest space,
> made of gold and clear
> deep light, and happy spirits far from fear.[159]

This is the familiar scholastic heaven that is motionless, devoid of living matter, and filled with light.

In another poem, however, Fray Luis uses classical images of a pastoral paradise to describe heaven. Gone is the light-filled scholastic heaven and in its place are Christianised Elysian Fields. In the *Dwelling Place of Heaven* (*Morada del Cielo*), Christ the Good Shepherd plays his rebec in sweet pastures to his sheep. Although the images of mountains, meadows, and fountains recall pagan themes of the Golden Age, Fray Luis makes the poem Christian by employing traditional mystical images. The 'sheep' do not merely hear the sounds; instead, the 'immortal sweetness stabs their soul', and they are plunged into the divine.[160] Consequently, although the starkness of the luminous scholastic heaven is avoided, the mystical union of soul with the divine is maintained. The soul's entire attention is still directed toward God, even if God is now portrayed as the gentle shepherd serenading his sheep rather than the ever-blazing fire of the empyrean.

The two images of empyrean and Elysium are skilfully merged in *Serene Night* (*Noche Serena*). The poem begins with Fray Luis' contemplation of the night sky and his unfortunate earthly existence. He is caught by the symmetry and brilliance of the heavens and remarks on the various celestial spheres, which circle the earth. Eventually he contemplates the highest heaven, the empyrean, with its typically scholastic characteristics of 'immeasurable beauty' and 'pure light', expressed in elegant rhyme: *inmensa hermosura, luz pura*.[161] But then, as if to temper the harsh brilliance of the beatific vision, he switches to pastoral imagery and concludes the poem with classical themes:

> O meadows! O sweet field
> of truth, fresh, redolent with pleasure! Springs
> from deepest veins revealed!
> O swollen hills and rings
> of hidden values filled with all good things![162]

---

159 Luis de León, *To Felipe Ruiz*, str. 14 (Luis de León, *The Unknown Light*, p. 75).
160 Luis de León, *Morada del Cielo*, str. 6 (Luis de León, *The Unknown Light*, p. 87).
161 Luis de León, *Noche Serena*, str. 14 and 15 (Luis de León, *The Unknown Light*, p. 62).
162 Luis de León, *Noche Serena*, str. 16 (Luis de León, *The Unknown Light*, p. 63).

Even when Fray Luis includes the classical imagery of *locus amoenus* (pleasant place) he is careful not to stray too far from accepted scholastic perspectives on heaven. As a victim of the Inquisition – he spent almost five years in a jail cell – Fray Luis knew better than to allow his poetic imagination and his mystical tendencies to lead him too far from standard medieval depictions of heaven. But neither should we think that he was really tempted to abandon theocentric notions of the afterlife. Mystics were actually their most loyal supporters.

Catholic popular culture

Popular Spanish Catholicism shows little interest in speculating about the details of life after death. The reason can be summed up in two slogans: 'heaven is far away', and 'heaven is the source of help'.

'Heaven is far away' – for each individual has a long way to go until he may arrive, one day, in heaven. First of all there is the present life with all its challenges and sufferings. Spanish Catholics have a long tradition of venerating suffering saints. The intense devotion to the passion of Christ, which began in the late sixteenth century in Spain and spread through the Spanish-speaking New World, presents the Saviour as the tortured suffering servant, and not the king of heaven.[163] The brotherhood of flagellants who beat themselves in memory of the passion and for the remission of their sins, the bloody statues of Christ, and the crosses dragged through Spanish towns during Holy Week processions all focus on the pain and humiliation of the Saviour.[164] Although the glorious resurrection is implied by the crucifixion, the symbols used in the cult of the passion associate the suffering of believers with the suffering of Christ. Spaniards do not have a comparable devotion to the resurrection, with its promise of eternal life. Even devotion to Mary tends to focus on her role as Sorrowful Mother and not on that as queen of heaven.

Once earthly life is over, the Spanish Catholic expects to enter the heavenly courtroom – the tribunal where ultimate justice is administered. Although intercessors such as the Virgin Mary or another saint may come to the aid of the soul, the divine sentence to be passed consigns even good persons to purgatory, and only very few souls – those of true saints – to heaven. For most people,

---

163 For the influence of Spanish piety in Mexico, see Jaime Lara, 'Christian Cannibalism and Human(e) Sacrifice: The Passion in the Conversion of the Aztecs', in: Christine E. Joynes (ed.), *Perspectives on the Passion*, London 2007, pp.139–165.
164 William A. Christian, *Local Religion in Sixteenth-Century Spain*, Princeton 1981, p. 185–201, 204–206.

explains Carlos Eire, elites and non-elites alike, death is 'not a journey from Madrid to heaven, so to speak, but from Madrid to purgatory'.[165] In purgatory they have to atone for their sins, before being admitted to heavenly glory. For many, this intermediate state becomes more of a concern than the goal itself. Spanish Catholicism historically has focused on purgatory: how to avoid getting there, how to lessen one's stay once one is there, and how to rescue unfortunate souls trapped there. Obtaining indulgences, which would limit time in purgatory, was a motivating factor for building monasteries, visiting churches, and having masses said. Religious brotherhoods devoted to the souls in purgatory became popular. Interest in the afterlife continues to be centred on the conditions of purgatory. Even for the pious individual, 'heaven is far away'.

But although heaven is far away, it is also a source of help. Folk beliefs, from the Middle Ages to the present day, weaken the boundaries between the natural world in which we now live and the world of the supernatural. Natural disasters such as droughts or plagues can both be caused by, and remedied by, supernatural forces. Religious vows taken by communities – vows promising permanent devotion to a saint, normally expressed by an annual celebration, in exchange for the saint's intercession with God – might protect the community against pestilence, hail, or locusts.[166] For much of Spanish history, life for the majority of people was precarious and often brutal. Speculation on the quality of life in heaven is not as compelling as speculating on how to address immediate, earthly concerns of hunger, shelter, and health. Consequently, folk Catholicism focuses more on bringing supernatural goodwill down to earth rather than describing what one might eventually see in heaven. Saints and angels come to earth and speak with human beings; people do not travel to heaven to speak to the angels. Miraculous apparitions – of the Virgin Mary, the saints, Christ – help people by allowing the sacred to touch both their lives and the natural order. Such visions do not convey information about the other world but rather tell the people what to do on earth: to build a shrine, to revere a certain relic, to wear a special emblem. Heavenly visitors journey to earth, but residents of the earth do not travel to heaven.

Throughout Spanish history, the community of saints in heaven and the living community on earth reached out towards one another. The two communities form an extended family where all the members are involved with each other. In intensely Catholic countries, such as Spain, the believers and the saints are intimately tied together. In Protestant countries, where the power of the saints has been devalued and the scholastic heaven challenged, a vacuum has been left

---

165 Eire, *From Madrid to Purgatory*, p. 15.
166 Christian, *Local Religion*, pp. 23–69.

in the understanding of heaven. Spanish Catholics know that heaven is populated by the Trinity, and Mary and the saints – the latter being sacred characters that periodically come to earth and who respond to human petitions. For Protestants, who do not revere Mary and the saints in the same way, the question becomes who is in heaven and what they do there. Speculation in Protestant circles on heavenly life has become much more vigorous than in Catholic circles. For many Protestants individual deceased family members comprise the heavenly communities. Since orthodox Protestant thought does not permit them to actively intervene in the affairs of the living, as Catholic saints did, these families are isolated in the other world of heaven. Consequently, Protestants living on earth more frequently travel to heaven either through visions, poetic reverie, or in theological speculation. Spanish Catholics, on the other hand, more often experience what historians of religion call a hierophany: the breaking of the sacred into the sphere of everyday life.

Hierophanies in the form of apparitions and miracles were much loved by the people; but they were also controlled by ecclesiastical authorities, especially by the Holy Office of the Inquisition, an institution established in 1478 with jurisdiction extending over the whole of Spain. As reports of such occurrences multiplied, the inquisitors decided to put an end to them. They were no longer willing to recognise them as genuine manifestations of the other world.

One example of inquisitorial intervention is the case of Francisca la Brava, a twenty-five-year-old woman living with her husband, a poor wool-carder, in the town of Quintanar in the province of Toledo. In October 1523 she reported to a priest, but also to women in her neighbourhood, her repeated nightly apparitions of the Virgin Mary, who spoke to her, telling her to collect alms for various churches and have Masses said for the dead. Among the angels who accompanied the Virgin, she recognised one of her sons who had died.[167] As news of the incident spread through the town, the inquisitors heard of the matter and investigated. The woman was tried before the Inquisition, the apparition was declared a frivolous invention, and the seer was sentenced to punishment. To make her an example to others, she was led through the streets on an ass, naked from the waist up, and given one hundred lashes.[168] This public humiliation was inflicted on her not once, but twice, in different towns. The incident illustrates the increased clerical control over what could have developed into one aspect of lay perspectives on heaven – the idea that the purity of young children would

---

167 William A. Christian, *Apparitions in Late Medieval and Renaissance Spain*, Princeton 1981, p. 177.
168 Christian, *Apparitions*, p. 179.

ensure their passage to heaven, sparing them the pains of purgatory.[169] The historian William Christian notes that the number of reports of apparitions declined dramatically after the 1520s with the flourishing of the Inquisition.[170] Nevertheless, we do hear of visions even after that date. Thus upon the death of Teresa of Avila in 1582, a nun at Valladolid saw a vision in which Teresa and St Francis of Assisi appeared together in heaven.[171]

How in more recent times ecclesiastical authorities and theologians have sought to promote theocentric views of the other world can be seen from what may be called a borderline case. In the 1860s, the Catholic world was swept by a small popular and bestselling book on heavenly reunions after death. Presented in the form of sentimental letters of consolation, the French Jesuit François-René Blot assured a widow that she would soon meet her husband again in heaven. Translated into many languages, this book was also made available in Spanish. The original title was *Au Ciel on se reconnaît. Lettres de consolation* (1863). The title used in English editions remained close to the original: *In Heaven We Know Our Own*. This in not the case with the Spanish edition: *Los lazos del Cielo – de Jesucristo con sus elegidos, de estos entre sí y del paraíso con la tierra: cartas de consuelo* (Madrid 1864), 'The ties of heaven: a study of the bonds between Jesus and his elect, between these, and between paradise and the earth. Letters of consolation.' This carefully phrased, lengthy but very guarded description obscures Father Blot's central message; by introducing the figure of Christ and mentioning him first, the title is given a theocentric slant. Spanish Catholics were not prevented from reading this Jesuit's book, but they were told not to forget that heaven is actually about Christ.

The conclusion, then, is clear enough: like the influence of Islam and the mystics' devotion to God alone, popular Catholicism in medieval and early-modern Spain was no seedbed of change toward an anthropocentric heaven. From this analysis, Spanish culture emerges as one in which theocentric orthodoxy remained firmly established.

Concluding observations

After our long journey through many previous centuries of Spanish cultural history, we can now return to more recent times and to the Jesuit Cándido Pozo,

---

169 Christian, *Apparitions*, p. 219.
170 Christian, *Apparitions*, p. 8.
171 Eire, *From Madrid to Purgatory*, pp. 213–214. This author devotes an entire chapter to Teresa's apparitions (pp. 472–501).

who in his 1992 manual on life after death portrays heaven in strictly theocentric terms. Interestingly, Pozo more than once invokes Miguel de Unamuno (1864–1936), one of the foremost philosophers, essayists and novelists of Spanish expression, as an authority, or at least as someone whose opinion he should consider and discuss. Indeed, Unamuno's thought on life after death does merit attention, especially as it is revealed in his famous book *The Tragic Sense of Life* (1913). Analysing the human soul, Unamuno discerns two competing tensions, those of unity and individuality. The soul yearns to be dissolved in the divine, yet at the same time seeks to maintain its unique separateness and personality. The mystical theocentricism of Teresa of Avila is cited as evidence for the wish for dissolution, while the visions of the Protestant seer Emanuel Swedenborg (1688–1772) are used to support belief in the maintenance of individual consciousness after death. The heavens of Swedenborg are dominated by the activities of the saints who married, educated children, and enjoyed the heavenly state as fully as their personalities would allow. Swedenborg had mystically travelled to heaven and seen a variety of societies filled with movement, change, and diversity.

For Unamuno heaven has to contain both mystical union and individual consciousness. 'Our fundamental feeling', Unamuno writes, 'is our longing not to lose the sense of the continuity of our consciousness, not to break the linkage of our memories, the sense of our own concrete identity, even though we may gradually be absorbed into Him, thus enhancing Him.'[172] Unamuno recognises that the union of the soul with the divine would eliminate individuality, change, and consciousness. Consequently, Unamuno explains that his soul longs not for absorption, quiescence, and extinction, but for a type of eternal purgatory, an eternal ascension. 'We must believe in the other life', he concludes, 'in the eternal life beyond the tomb, and in an individual and personal life, a life in which each one of us senses his own consciousness and senses that it is joined, without being confounded, with all others in their consciousness within the Supreme Consciousness, in God.'[173] For Unamuno, the beatific vision is not the 'contemplation of the supreme Truth, whole and entire', but rather the 'continuous discovery of it all'.[174] No soul can immediately know the divine and preserve any of its unique consciousness. In order for the personal consciousness to be forever active, knowledge must come not immediately but gradually. Heaven must have room for both God and the individual.

---

172 Miguel de Unamuno, *The Tragic Sense of Life*. Translated by Anthony Kerrigan, Princeton 1972, p. 250.
173 Unamuno, *The Tragic Sense of Life*, p. 281.
174 Unamuno, *The Tragic Sense of Life*, p. 250.

To compensate for the abstract – and abstruse – nature of his philosophical argument in the chapter 'Religion, mythology of the beyond, and apocatastasis', Unamuno in a later chapter supplies a more graphic and emotional portrait of the other world. He comments on the final chivalric adventure of Don Quixote as follows:

> Don Quixote, then, died and went down into hell, which he entered, lance on rest, and there he freed all the condemned, as he had freed the galley slaves, and he closed the gates of hell, and took down the inscription Dante saw there, 'Abandon all hope!', and replaced it with one reading 'Long live hope'. And then, escorted by the souls he had freed, and they laughing at him, he went to heaven. And God laughed paternally at him, and this divine laughter filled his soul with eternal felicity.[175]

Don Quixote, himself a symbol of hope, assumes in this episode the role of Christ who descends into the netherworld in order to release all those who were there. Yet the heaven of Don Quixote remains, on the whole, theocentric, despite the fatherly laughter of God and the companionship of the redeemed.

In 1913 Unamuno wrote that 'we must believe in that other life in order to live this life and endure it, and endow it with meaning and purpose'.[176] This sounds like a recipe for modern spirituality, and at the same time like a summary of how Unamuno felt about life. His short story *Saint Manuel Bueno, Martyr* (1930), however, points in a different direction, indicating, it seems, a heightened sense of what the philosopher calls the tragic sense of life. The hero of the story, a country priest who has lost all belief in life after death, reveals his unbelief to just a few, but not to the simple folks – for they need their religious beliefs, including the expectation of meeting their family in the other world, because it gives them a sense of meaning and stability. In order to help people live, Don Manuel – this priest – continues to preach the doctrines that he secretly no longer holds valid. As a result, he suffers. Apparently, unbelief is only for the minority of those prepared to confront the shocking and tragic truth about our human existence. The truth, the priest explains, 'is perhaps something terrible, something unbearable, something deadly; simple people would not be able to live with it'.[177]

In 1988 the Centro de Investigaciones Sociológicas in Madrid published the results of its study on religious beliefs in Spain. The findings sharply contradict the expectations one might have upon reading Unamuno's novel, for only 45%

---

175 Unamuno, *The Tragic Sense of Life*, p. 351, in the chapter 'Don Quixote in contemporary tragicomedy'.
176 Unamuno, *The Tragic Sense of Life*, p. 281.
177 Miguel de Unamuno, *Saint Manuel Bueno, Martyr – San Manuel Bueno, mártir*. Translated by Paul Burns and Salvador Ortiz-Carboneres, Oxford 2009, p. 79 (text of the short story in Spanish and English).

of those surveyed believed in the existence of heaven.[178] Accordingly, the majority has lost its traditional beliefs in life after death. Other statistics available for Spain give slightly higher figures for believers – 60% (1995) and 51% (2000).[179] For the sake of comparison, one may quote the relevant figures for France – 31% (2000), Great Britain – 56% (2000), East Germany – 14% (2000), West Germany – 35% (2000), and the United States – 87% (2000).[180] To explain why so many of the Spanish no longer believe in heaven, while 87 % of all Americans still do, exceeds the scope of this essay. But this much can be said: for many Spaniards, as for many other Europeans, belief in heaven no longer appears to be an essential ingredient for finding meaning in this life.

---

178 Centro de Investigaciones Sociológicas, *Estudios y Encuestas* 11 (June 1988): 'Relaciones interpersonales, actitudes y valores en la Espāna de los ochenta'.
179 Loek Halman et al., *Changing Values and Beliefs in 85 Countries*, Leiden 2008, p. 223.
180 Halman et al., *Changing Values and Beliefs in 85 Countries*, p. 223.

Chapter 5: A Swedish Heaven. Swedenborg on *Heaven and Hell* (1758) – Appendix: Swedenborg Chronology

> But I again repeat my conviction, that Swedenborg's *Meaning* is the truth – and the duty of his followers is, to secure this meaning to the Readers of his works by collecting from his numerous Volumes those passages, in which this meaning is conveyed in terms so plain as not to be misconceived: an introduction of 50 pages would suffice for this purpose.[181]
> Samuel Taylor Coleridge, marginal note on Swedenborg, *De Coelo*

Emanuel Swedenborg (1688–1772) was a man with two careers: one in science and one in theology. The first career ended in 1747 when he retired from his position on the Royal Board of Mines in his home country, Sweden. With inherited resources augmented by a small salary, the fifty-nine-year-old scholar went abroad, spending much time in London and Amsterdam, cities he knew from earlier visits. London was where, in April 1745, he had had a vision of 'the Lord God, the Creator of the world and the Redeemer', who permitted him to see 'the worlds of spirits, heaven, and hell'.[182] He later devoted all of his time and energy to the writing of theological books. His initial endeavours came to fruition in 1756 with the publication of the eighth and final tome of *Arcana coelestia, quae in Scriptura Sacra, seu Verbo Domini sunt detecta: Una cum Mirabilibus quae Visa Sunt in Mundo Spirituum, et in Coelo Angelorum* (A Disclosure of Secrets of Heaven, Contained in Sacred Scripture, or the Word of the Lord. Together with Amazing Things Seen in the World of Spirits and in the Heaven of Angels). At the express will of the writer, the volumes bore no indication of authorship. Completed in his sixty-eighth year, they constitute Swedenborg's foundational theological work.

The learned author could then have retired for good, for on all accounts, he had achieved a great deal. Moreover, after all these years of writing, he must

---

181 Samuel Taylor Coleridge, *The Collected Works.* Vol. 12/5: *Marginalia.* Edited by H. J. Jackson and George Whalley, Princeton 2000, p. 410. On Coleridge's interest in Swedenborg, see H.J. Jackson, 'Swedenborg's Meaning is the Truth: Coleridge, Tulk, and Swedenborg', in: *In Search of the Absolute: Essays on Swedenborg and Literature.* Edited by Stephen McNeilly, London 2004, pp. 1–13.
182 Rudolf Leonhard Tafel, *Documents concerning the Life and Character of Emanuel Swedenborg*, London 1875, vol. 1, p. 36. An analysis of this vision and the problems of the authenticity of the relevant report can be found in Ernst Benz, in: Emanuel Swedenborg, *Ausgewählte religiöse Schriften*, Marburg 1949, pp, 278–288.

have been exhausted, or so one would think. In fact, this was not the case. Swedenborg must have felt that a work of eight huge quarto tomes of biblical exegesis, theological reflection, and reports on the author's visions would not find many readers, at least not immediately. So he prepared a number of smaller, less forbidding books, some of which were closely based on *Arcana Coelestia*. Five of these appeared in 1758, shortly after the author's seventieth birthday.[183] All were in Latin, printed in London by John Lewis who had a bookshop in Paternoster Row.[184] They also appeared anonymously and drew heavily on *Arcana coelestia*, to which they seem intended to draw attention. These new, shorter books were based mainly on certain sections of *Arcana coelestia* in which particular theological subjects were systematically developed, standing out in contrast to the primary focus of the book, which is a running commentary on Genesis and Exodus.

One of these smaller books of 1758 was titled *De Coelo et ejus mirabilibus, et de Inferno, ex audits et visis* (Heaven and Its Wonders and Hell, Drawn from Things Heard and Seen).[185] Apparently one thousand copies were printed.[186] Designed as a kind of introduction to some of the ideas of *Arcana coelestia*, it was short, concise, and well organized; the pedagogical aim is visible throughout in the uncomplicated Latin style, the frequent announcements of what will be discussed next, and the summaries that punctuate the book. Swedenborg himself annotated the book with references to *Arcana coelestia* and appended to individual chapters summaries of certain subjects dealt with in that work (for example, after no. 86), so that the reader is constantly reminded of the larger work. As an introductory text based on a more comprehensive theological work,

---

183 Swedenborg was not the only author to produce an abridgement of his *Arcana Coelestia* in his own time. In southern Germany, Friedrich Christoph Oetinger (1702–1782), a Lutheran minister, deplored the inaccessibility of the huge Latin quarto tomes, and in 1765 published a hundred-page summary: Friedrich Christoph Oetinger, *Swedenborgs und anderer irdische und himmlische Philosophie*, Reutlingen 1855, part 1, pp. 15–116.

184 Alfred Acton, *The Letters and Memorials of Emanuel Swedenborg*, Bryn Athyn, Penn. 1955, vol. 2, p. 523.

185 Throughout this chapter, we use *De Coelo* as a shorthand for *De Coelo et ejus Mirabilibus, et de Inferno*. As is common in Swedenborgian studies, text citations refer not to page numbers but to Swedenborg's section numbers, which appear in the original edition of 1758 and in all subsequent editions and translations. In this study, section numbers refer to *De Coelo* and its English translation by the paragraph numbers used in the original Latin edition of 1758. In this study, section numbers where no work is specified should be understood to refer to *De Coelo*. Thus 'no. 90' means '*De Coelo*, no. 90'. The authoritative English translation is: Swedenborg, *Heaven and Its Wonders and Hell. Drawn from Things Heard and Seen*. Translated by George F. Dole (The New Century Edition of the Works of Emanuel Swedenborg), West Chester, Penn. 2000.

186 Acton, *The Letters and Memorials of Emanuel Swedenborg*, vol. 2, p. 524.

De Coelo forms part of a larger corpus of texts. Occasionally Swedenborg also refers to other writings such as *De Nova Hierosolyma et Ejus Doctrina Coelesti* (The New Jerusalem and Its Heavenly Teaching, see *De Coelo*, no. 78) and *De Ultimo Judicio, et de Babylonia Destructa* (The Last Judgment and the Destruction of Babylon; see *De Coelo*, no. 559), both belonging to the same series of books printed in 1758. Although meant as an accessible introduction for 'church people these days' and, specifically, for 'people of simple heart and simple faith' (no. 1), *De Coelo* is not a work complete in itself, and any thorough study must take account of this fact. What Swedenborg really means, one might say, can only be found out by examination of the entire corpus, not by consideration of just one small, isolated part of it. Recognising the importance of the context of *De Coelo,* the English romantic author Samuel Taylor Coleridge (1772–1834) scribbled in the margin of his Latin copy the comment cited in the epigraph above. In what follows here, however, the incompleteness of *De Coelo* is not emphasised, for doing so would detract from its value, especially for first-time readers. Instead, *De Coelo* is examined as a representative fragment that echoes and conveys the spirit and meaning of Swedenborg's theological *oeuvre*. It is viewed here as if it were a complete work, the contents of which can be treated as a coherent presentation of the author's teaching.

De Coelo's map of the universe

The best way to summarise the contents of *De Coelo* is to reconstruct its teaching in the form of a schematic map of the universe (Fig. 5.1). The material world (*mundus*) in which we live, is only a small part within the whole. Surrounded by vast spiritual worlds, it is comparable to a small principality surrounded by extensive empires. The first of these empires is the *mundus spirituum* (no. 421), the world of the spirits of the dead. Immediately after death, people find themselves in this region. After some time, they either sink down into the infernal regions (*inferna*, the hells) or they rise up to heaven. Heaven has a complex structure that echoes the human form. It is differentiated into three heavens: the first or outermost heaven, the second or middle heaven, and the third or inmost heaven. Each heaven contains innumerable communities, and each community, many angels. The structure of hell is similar to that of heaven, although inverted. Each community in hell is balanced by a community in heaven devoted to a corresponding form of love. The entire structure is encompassed and animated by the Lord (*Dominus*).[187]

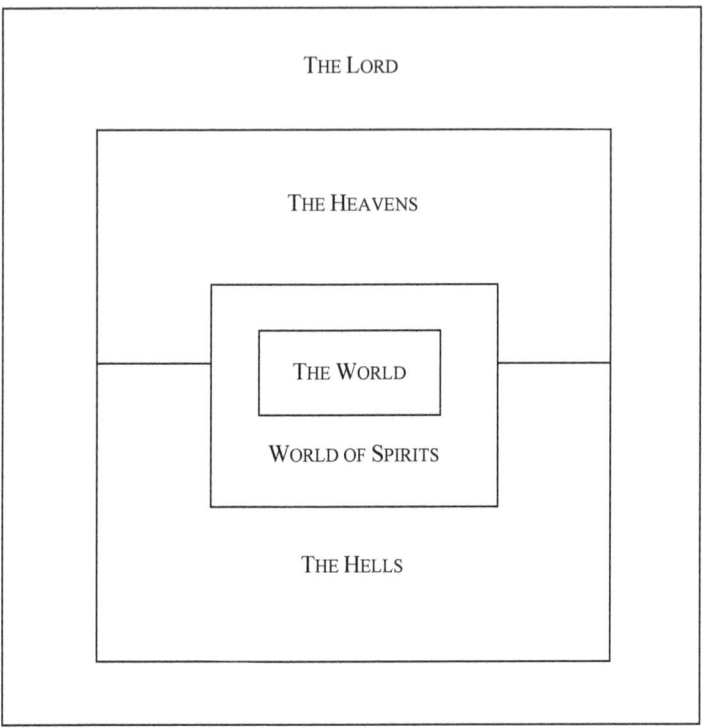

5.1 *Swedenborg's Map of the Universe (first version).* – *In De Coelo, Swedenborg describes the various realms that make up the universe. This description could be presented schematically in various ways. The diagram suggested here sets our world at the centre of the realms, with the Lord framing and encompassing the whole.*

---

187 Heaven (*coelum*, or in the plural, *coela*), also called the spiritual world (*mundus spiritualis*, no. 114), is divided into three sections. Swedenborg explains that the lowest realm is the natural heaven (*coelum naturale, no. 31); higher up, it is followed by the spiritual kingdom (*regnum spirituale*, no. 21) and the heavenly kingdom (*regnum coeleste*, no. 21). Hell is divided in two sections: an upper hell called the region of the spirits (*regnum spirituum, no. 596) and a lower, gloomier hell called the region of the demons (*regnum geniorum, no. 596). Swedenborg's thought is generally clear, but he does not aim at complete terminological consistency. For the sake of clarity, we use certain terms – such as *regnum geniorum* and *coelum naturale* – that are not actually used in Swedenborg's text but stay close to his description; in this note they are marked with an asterisk (*).

Figure 5.1 Swedenborg's map of the universe (first version). In *De Coelo*, Swedenborg describes the various realms that make up the universe. This description could be schematised in various ways. The schema suggested here sets our world at the centre of the realms; it should be contrasted with figure 5.2.

In *De Coelo*, Swedenborg describes his map of the universe starting with the top level, so that after commenting on God, he deals with heaven, then the realm of the spirits, and eventually with hell, the lowest level. Our world, that is, the central area, is not described in a separate section, but referred to whenever necessary. But as soon as the map is understood, one can open Swedenborg's book anywhere and start reading wherever one pleases. The following description departs from Swedenborg's approach by starting with the map's central realm – our world – and then moving toward the realms that encompass it: the world of spirits, heaven, hell, and eventually the Lord as the ultimate reality.

The World

The world (*mundus*), located at the centre of the structure, is the material world in which we live. This world is composed of numerous earths, scattered through the universe, of which our globe is merely one (no. 417). All the earths are peopled with human beings.[188] For practical purposes, however, it suffices to equate the world with our earth alone. On earth, we find the church, defined as 'the Lord's heaven on earth' (no. 57). In the world, the Christian church is responsible for teaching people the proper worldview – that is, all about the various spiritual worlds surrounding and encompassing the *mundus*. However, the traditional churches have generally failed. Swedenborg refers to the world quite frequently, for whatever he explains is for the knowledge and the benefit of those living in this realm. In structural terms, one important feature of the world is its location between heaven and hell. Both of these realms try to influence the world and impinge upon individual lives; as a result, the two forces neutralise each other, so that humans are free – neither forced to submit to evil nor forced to yield to good (nos. 597–602). They can freely decide between good and evil.

---

188 On this subject, see Swedenborg's book *De Telluribus in mundo nostro solari, quae vocantur planetae*, 1758. See Bernhard Lang, 'Auch noch andere Menschen und andre Geschlechter der Tiere: Menschliches Leben im außerirdischen Weltall in der Sicht von Fontenelle (1686), Huygens (1698) und Swedenborg (1758)', in Thomas P. Weber (ed.), *Science & Fiction II. Leben auf anderen Sternen*, Frankfurt 2004, pp. 13–40, 255–258. Swedenborg imagines some of the planets being populated by human creatures that resemble Africans or American Indians.

In our diagram, we have taken care to include one aspect emphasised by Swedenborg: the influence of heaven and hell on our world is not direct, but is exercised through spirits active in their own world (no. 600).

In a world of freedom of choice, moral guidance is imperative. Swedenborg has much to say and to recommend about right and wrong living in the world, and he offers his advice. Central themes relate to work, marriage, and churchgoing. An active, productive life of service to society counts as the ideal. Swedenborg warns of idleness and asceticism. Idleness never makes one happy (no. 403), and withdrawal from active life, for instance in monastic communities, tends to inflate people with a sense of their own worth, thus leading away from association with those divine forces necessary to happiness both here and hereafter (no. 535). As for marriage, *De Coelo* warns against any domineering attitude in the conjugal relationship, for 'any love of control of one over the other utterly destroys marital love' (no. 380). The book also warns against marriage between partners of divergent religions, because true marital love cannot develop between them (no. 378). Even an interpretation of conjugal intimacy is offered: 'Marital pleasure, which is a purer and more delicate pleasure of touch, surpasses all others because of its service, the procreation of the human race and thus of the angelic heaven' (no. 402). Concerning religion, Swedenborg pronounces a verdict on those who think constant churchgoing and praying would be the right path (no. 535). He knows the limitations and spiritual dangers of what outwardly appears to be a holy and devout life. In sum, the seer's ethical message is one of optimism: 'It is not so hard to lead a heaven-bound life as people think it is' (title nos. 528–535).

While still living in the material world (*mundus*), Swedenborg was granted glimpses of the vast realms that transcend and encompass the earthly realm. While in the Middle Ages Dante could present his worldview in the form of a coherent narrative, Swedenborg prefers a more systematic, philosophical description. At many points, however, his description includes autobiographical narrative statements: as a visionary, Swedenborg conversed with the residents of the other regions. There is nothing strange about this communication, Swedenborg assures us, for all the beings he encounters are people who once lived a normal human life in this world.

The World of Spirits

The world of spirits (*mundus spirituum*) is the realm immediately encasing our material world. Swedenborg's observations about this region can be found under the heading 'The World of Spirits and Our State after Death' (nos. 421–535). As this heading indicates, death shifts people's primary consciousness from the material world (*mundus*) to the world of spirits (*mundus spirituum*). During their stay in this intermediary world, people go through various stages:

1. The first stage can be described as one of introduction. Having arrived in this world, people seem to be still the same. They meet the same way as in their earthly lives –'we can talk to anyone when we want to, to friends and acquaintances from our physical life, especially husbands and wives, and also brothers and sisters. I have seen a father talking with his six sons and recognizing them. I have seen many other people with their relatives and friends', reports the visionary (no. 427).
2. The second stage is one of transformation. People meet angels – formerly real human beings, delegated from heaven to offer instruction about the Lord, heavenly existence, and the values of goodness and truth (no. 548). Exposed to such angelic teaching, people increasingly focus on their basic spiritual attitude so that their positive or negative character asserts itself. People sort out their true thoughts, feelings, and attitudes, and so reveal their true nature. Some good people's personalities are found to include certain crude and false elements of thought and orientation. After a purgatory-like period of suffering, they can be reckoned among the good (no. 513). Eventually, people change. They shed the form of the physical body that they inherited from their parents, so that their own, individual, previously concealed inner form becomes visible, a form shaped by their true nature, character, and orientation. People of a good character now have lovely faces, while people of evil orientation have ugly ones (no. 457).
3. Having reached their definitive form at the end of the second stage, the good and the wicked part company to lead their own lives. The wicked ones can leave the world of spirits immediately, sinking headlong down into hell. The good ones, by contrast, go through one more stage of angelic instruction that prepares them for heavenly existence (no. 512).

Although some people stay for a long time in the world of spirits – up to thirty years – most of the newcomers soon find their way either up to heaven or down into hell (no. 426). Which way one goes depends on the inner orientation that one has acquired during one's earthly existence and that has asserted itself in response to angelic instruction. Evil people choose hell, good people, heaven.

Heaven

De Coelo devotes most space to describing heaven and heavenly existence (nos. 20–420). Although much of the text relies on abstract psychological and philosophical notions and may seems impenetrable to first-time readers, many have been attracted to and charmed by the seer's lively descriptions of the world of the angels. The angels, according to Swedenborg, are none other than the blessed ones – those people who, having lived their lives in the world (*mundus*) and having then spent some time in the world of spirits (*mundus spirituum*), have found their permanent abode in one of the heavenly kingdoms. Speaking of all humans, Swedenborg explains that 'We have been created to enter heaven and become angels' (*homo creatus est ut in coelum veniat, & fiat Angelus*, no. 57).

Whereas many people think of angels as 'minds without form', as 'something airy with something alive within it', Swedenborg insists on their truly human form (no. 74). 'They have faces, eyes, ears, chests, arms, hands, and feet. They see each other, hear each other, and talk to each other. In short, they lack nothing that belongs to humans except that they are not clothed with a material body' (no. 75). Like his father, the Lutheran Bishop Jesper Swedberg (1653–1735), Swedenborg insists that the inhabitants of heaven are not deprived of the most elementary means of communication, language.[189] 'Angels talk to each other just as we do in this world. They discuss various things – domestic matters, community concerns, issues of moral life, and issues of spiritual life', the seer explains (no. 234). He adds that 'angelic language, like human language, is differentiated into words. It is similarly uttered audibly and heard aurally' (no. 235). While his father had speculated that the Swedes would speak Swedish in heaven, but would understand other languages without difficulty, Swedenborg advances the more philosophical view that 'all people in heaven have the same language', no matter where they come from (no. 236).

In heaven, like-natured and like-minded angels recognised each other easily, and so they come together to form communities (*societates*). Swedenborg's description sounds very much like a description of cities, towns, and villages on earth: the larger forms of these communities consist of tens of thousands of individuals, the smaller of some thousands, and the smallest of hundreds. Some people live alone (no. 50). The seer repeatedly insists on the fact that the communities are not formed by a law imposed from outside; rather, each heavenly community is constituted by the inner being of every member. In

---

189 For Jesper Swedberg's interest in the language of the saints, see Martin Lamm, *Swedenborg. Eine Studie zu seiner Entwicklung zum Mystiker und Geisterseher*. Translated by I. Meyer-Lüne, Leipzig 1922, p. 5.

Swedenborg's words: 'Heaven is not outside angels but within them' (no. 53). The members of the heavenly communities live in houses; these are 'just like the houses on earth that we call homes, but more beautiful. They have chambers, suites, and bedrooms in abundance, and courtyards with gardens, flower beds, and lawns around them' (no. 184). The houses form cities with streets and lanes and public squares 'just like the ones we see in cities on our earth' (no. 184).

As former men and women, the angels are male and female (no. 366). As a consequence, they form couples. Mate is drawn toward mate when their minds can be united into one. They fall in love at first sight and enter into marriage. With many people gathered around them, they also hold a feast in celebration of their union (no. 383). The Lord blesses their mutual love and makes them happy. Heavenly couples differ from their earthly counterparts only in that they have no children (no. 382b).

Does heavenly bliss consist of a life of leisure? No, answers the seer, for idleness never leads to happiness (no. 403). Far from being idle, heavenly life is an active life. Ecclesiastic, civic, and domestic affairs all keep the angels busy not only within their own society (no. 388), but also beyond it. As a rule, each heavenly society is assigned specific duties. The inhabitants of some work as guardian angels in the world; their task is leading people away from evil feelings and thoughts and helping them to control their deeds (no. 391). Others work among the spirits that have newly arrived in the world of spirits. Yet others raise the children who have died in infancy. Swedenborg assures all grieving parents that 'all children, whether born within or outside the church, are adopted by the Lord and become angels' (no. 416).

Hell

The infernal regions (*inferna*), with their division into an upper level called the region of spirits (*regnum spirituum*) and a lower one called the region of demons (*regnum geniorum*, see no. 596), are dealt with at length, though not nearly as extensively as the heavenly realms (nos. 536–588). The spirits (*spiritûs*) and demons (*genii*) are none other than former human beings. According to Swedenborg, there are no devils and demons which other Christians believe to be spiritual beings made by God in a separate act of creation; this common belief, Swedenborg says, is quite unjustified. Both the spirits and the demons have lived on earth, have died, and have spent some time in the world of spirits. Why are they in hell, a place of 'rank, foul stenches' (no. 429)? Swedenborg asserts that the reason sinners enter hell is not that the Lord is angry with them (no. 545).

They dwell there because during their earthly existence they preferred evil to good and thus associated themselves more and more with the infernal realms. As a result, they ended up in the region of evil spirits or, worse, in the region of demons.

What happens to the evil spirits and the demons in hell? No judgment based on records of past crimes and offences is passed by a court,[190] and there is no prison per se, no fire, no devil with a fork. Instead, the evil ones suffer from their own spiritual state (no. 547). We must beware, however, of misunderstanding Swedenborg: he does not minimise the tortures of hell by referring to them in psychological terms of inner unhappiness;[191] instead, he consistently describes the tortures of hell as harm inflicted from the outside. 'The hellish mob craves and loves nothing more than inflicting harm, especially inflicting punishment and torture' (no. 550). St Matthew's gospel describes hell as a place of utter darkness, of "weeping and gnashing of teeth" (Matthew 8:12), and the passage does easily lend itself to a psychological interpretation. Swedenborg specifically comments on the biblical text, but takes it to refer to 'clashes and battles' between the citizens of hell (no. 575). Unlike Swedenborg, his contemporary Jean-Jacques Rousseau (1712–1778) does come close to defining hell in psychological terms. According to book IV of *Emile*, human hearts are 'eaten away by envy, avarice, and ambition', so that hell is '*dans le coeur des méchants*' – in the hearts of the wicked.[192] Both Rousseau and Swedenborg consider wicked hearts and evil acts as intimately linked, and both know that evil originates in the human heart. Yet, despite this concurrence, Rousseau emphasises the role of the human heart in wickedness, while Swedenborg accentuates the importance of actions. Rousseau's hell can be described as incarceration in a mental asylum, whereas Swedenborg's inferno is a society ruled by the wicked. In hell, unconstrained by normal social mores, the wicked heart attempts to express itself freely in ever-new evil acts.

What about punishment? In Swedenborg's hell, punishment does exist, but it is never based on records of sins committed during earthly life. Instead, punishment is incurred exclusively for deeds perpetrated in hell (no. 509). It is inflicted by other demons who never miss a chance to persecute and torment others of their kind.

---

190 It should be observed that no. 462b, 7 comes uncharacteristically close to a suggestion of 'court proceedings'.
191 Inner agony (*dolor*), according to Swedenborg, is never a permanent state of unhappiness, but only a temporary state or feeling (see no. 400,3–4).
192 Jean-Jacques Rousseau, *Emile, or On Education* [1762]. Translated by A. Bloom, London 1991, p. 284.

The state in which the wicked find themselves depends on their individual urges and inner qualities (no. 508), all of which reflect love of self and love of the world in various degrees (no. 554). To the good, they appear as 'monsters' (no. 80) that are 'misshapen, black, and grotesque' in form (no. 99), wearing 'nothing but rags, dirty and foul' (no. 182). 'Some of their faces are black, some like little torches, some pimply, with huge ulcerated sores' (no. 553). But, Swedenborg asks, are they ultimately lost to heaven? Yes they are! It is definitely in this world, our world of time and space, that we can and must choose. Once the evil character of someone has asserted itself, there will be no more change, and so there will be no escape from hell, in all eternity. 'A great deal of experience has convinced me that after death we remain the same forever' (no. 480). Consequently, 'the people in the hells cannot be saved' (*non salvari possunt qui in Infernis*, no. 595). Yet Swedenborg holds out to those in hell a little hope: sometimes, the Lord sends angels to people in hell to prevent them from tormenting each other excessively (no. 391).

Swedenborg briefly describes the woeful condition and activities of the infernal spirits. Living in crude huts, the hellish spirits engage in 'constant quarrels, hostility, beating, and violence. The streets and alleys are full of thieves and robbers. In some hells there are nothing but brothels, foul to look at and full of all kinds of filth and excrement' (no. 586). The seer hints in one passage (no. 600) that they try to influence people living in the earthly realm. The most evil of spirits, the demons (*genii*), 'take particular delight in making themselves invisible and floating around people like ghosts, doing their harm covertly, spraying it around like the venom of snakes' (no. 578). Swedenborg indicates that the spirits also make assaults on heaven (no. 595), but to no avail; for when the heavens defend themselves against hell, the angels by a mere effort of will disperse evil spirits and cast them back into hell (no. 229). The result of this constant conflict and antagonism is a dynamic play. Supervised and regulated by the Lord, who always supports the heavenly forces, the interplay of antagonistic powers results in a great cosmic equilibrium (nos. 592, 593). Far from being in a sterile state of homeostasis, the universe teems with life.

The dynamic character of Swedenborg's universe emerges even more clearly when we compare it with traditional scholastic notions of the afterlife. According to much of Christian tradition, human life will eventually come to a halt in heaven and hell. Having reached its goal, it ceases to exist. In heaven, the blessed would be rewarded essentially by the beatific vision of God. In hell, the damned would be punished by eternal suffering. *De Coelo* would have none of this. Heaven, a dynamic reality, means harmonious life under divine influence, whereas hell means disharmonious life separate from the Lord. For the author of

De Coelo, human life will continue forever – both in this world and in the spiritual universes that surround it.

The Lord

All of this life comes from the Lord (*Dominus*) who encompasses and sustains the entire cosmic structure. Everything that exists and lives owes its being to the Lord, and indeed draws its power of being at any moment from the Lord (no. 9). Cut off from its source of being, everything would immediately vanish into nothingness. In the world (*mundus*), not all people turn to the Lord as to their source of being, but in the spiritual world, all the angels do. To the angels of the heavenly kingdom, he is visible as a sun high above the heavens (no. 118) – 'reddish and gleaming, so brilliant as to be beyond description' (no. 159).

The solar metaphor for the Lord is used in a way that gives Swedenborg's theocentric universe a heliocentric structure: 'Since the Lord is the sun of heaven [...] the Lord is the common centre (*Dominus est Centrum commune*)' (no. 124). Elsewhere Swedenborg uses more traditional expressions with a vertical dimension, according to which God is above everything else, and the various heavens are called lower and higher ones (no. 22). However, a close reading reveals that Swedenborg often switches his language from vertical to centric metaphors. Thus the higher angels and heavens are also called 'more inward' ones, i.e. those that are closer to the divine centre (nos. 22, 29, 31). 'All perfection increases as we move inward, and decreases as we move outward, because more inward things are closer to the Lord and intrinsically purer, while more outward things are more remote from the Lord and intrinsically cruder' (no. 34). Figure 5.2 is an attempt to visualize Swedenborg's centric description and offer an alternative to the previous map of his universe (Fig. 5.1).

Whereas the schema offered in fig. 5.1 places God (the Lord) at the periphery, so that he encompasses the universe, an alternative representation is implied in Swedenborg's text. The seer also speaks of the various levels of heaven as being closer to or farther from the divine centre. This schema places the Lord at the centre and relegates all else to the periphery.

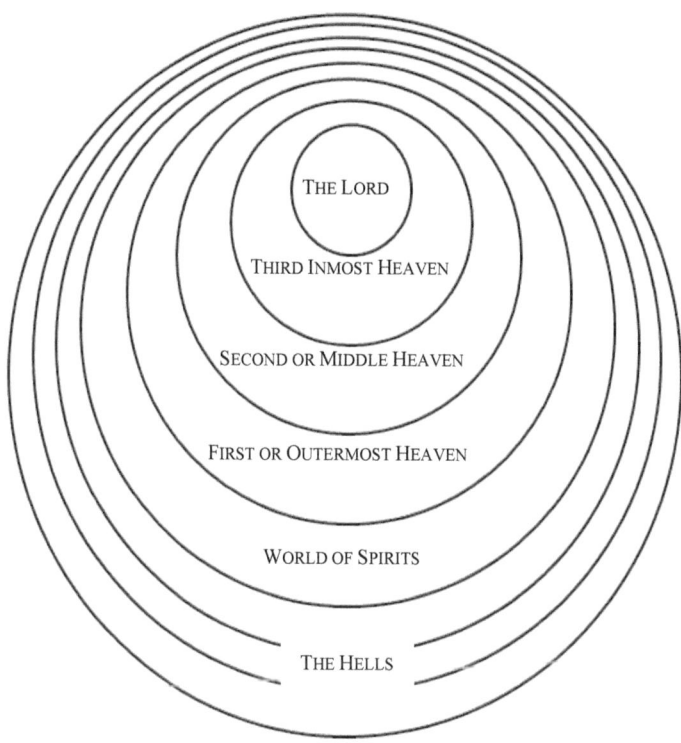

5.2 Swedenborg's Map of the Universe (second version). – The seer can speak of the various levels of heaven as being closer to or farther from the divine centre. Accordingly, this diagram places the Lord at the centre and relegates all else to the periphery.

Swedenborg takes care to correct common misunderstandings of the notion of God. According to him, theologians have often misrepresented the nature of the Lord by believing in three divine beings (no. 2) or by denying the divinity of the Lord while recognising only the Father (no. 3). There is only one Lord (or God), who manifested himself on earth as Jesus, and who manifests himself in heaven as the sun or the moon (nos. 117–118). He may also manifest himself in angelic – that is, human – form (nos. 55, 121). The Lord's self-manifestation and visibility are facts much emphasised by Swedenborg; only misguided philosophers think of God as invisible and, consequently, as incomprehensible (nos. 82, 86). Those who describe God as the invisible soul of the universe, a being beyond the grasp of human cognition (no. 3), are clearly mistaken. Read as a critique of this naturalistic philosophy, Swedenborg's *De Coelo* emerges as a celebration of the knowledge of divine realities. The seer was granted that knowledge in two mutually supportive ways – by way of direct mystical communication with angels and through being enabled to understand the inner meaning of the biblical writings. 'It has been granted to me to be with angels and to talk to them person to person', he explains. 'Now I am being allowed therefore to describe what I have heard and seen, in the hopes of shedding light where there is ignorance and dispelling scepticism' (no. 1).

Elements of interpretation

The words just cited are a solid starting point for an examination of the biographical and historical context of Swedenborg's visions. 'It has been granted to me to be with angels and to talk to them person to person. I have also been enabled to see what it is like in heaven and in hell, a process that has been going on for thirteen years' (no. 1). Since these words were written they have electrified many who had read or heard about them. During the last years of his life, Emanuel Swedenborg became a kind of celebrity, and people sought him out at home in Stockholm and London, or wherever they could find him. He did not mind being approached. One of his visitors, the German poet Gottlieb Friedrich Klopstock (1724–1803), wanted to be put in touch with his departed friends – which, however, Swedenborg refused to do.[193] Klopstock and many others considered him a medium or spirit-seer, and people wanted to hear him talk about angels or dead relatives, out of sheer curiosity. They relied on hearsay and, perhaps, on a very superficial reading of books like *De Coelo*, which seemed to them a conglomeration of disparate hallucinations. While it is true that Swedenborg did claim to be in contact with the other world, many contemporaries misunderstood him or simply overlooked that he wanted to lay the foundation of a new theology. They also were unaware of the sober, reasoned language and style of thought in *De Coelo*. Therefore the foregoing summary has sought to stress the systematic, coherent character of the book's teaching.

In what follows Swedenborg's teaching is examined from a different angle – a historical one. Historical understanding of a text that is as remote from our time and as complex as *De Coelo* demands inquiry into the various layers of its cultural, philosophical, and religious background. The metaphor of layers immediately makes sense when one considers that *Swedenborg's philosophy belongs to the eclectic tradition*. Today, eclecticism has a bad name, for it is applied to systems of thought that arbitrarily combine elements from a variety of

---

[193] Tafel, *Documents concerning the Life and Character of Emanuel Swedenborg*, London 1890, vol. 2/3, p. 697.

sources without adequate justification for the combination. In the seventeenth and eighteenth centuries by contrast, many philosophers and scientists celebrated eclecticism as the only adequate procedure. Truth, they claimed, cannot be attained by committing oneself wholeheartedly to any one traditional school such as the one founded by Plato (427–347 BCE), Aristotle (384–322 BCE), or the Stoics; it can only be found through experience and by carefully scrutinising and possibly refining received ideas and notions found in the huge repertoire of insight already accumulated. Tradition, in the form of received ideas, and innovation, in the form of new insights gained through experiment and careful observation, interacted to produce new knowledge. Eclectic minds were open to all sorts of ideas, combined these into ever new figurations, developed them in ever new ways, and rarely sought to trace – or to reveal – their ultimate sources.

In science, the golden age of eclecticism was around 1700, when in Germany Johann Christoph Sturm (1635–1704) ranked as its leading representative.[194] As a scholar of 'natural philosophy' (as it was then called), Sturm wrote about mathematics and physics, introduced experimental physics in the courses he taught in Altdorf (the university of Nuremberg, Bavaria), interacted with specialists like the English chemist Robert Boyle (1627–1691), and caught the attention of the German philosopher Gottfried Wilhelm Leibniz (1646–1716). Sturm explained his approach in a treatise titled *De philosophia sectaria et electiva* (1679, On Sectarian and Eclectic Philosophy) and called his later collection of papers *Philosophia eclectica* (1686, 1698; Eclectic Philosophy). In order to make up one's mind about natural phenomena, Sturm insisted, it is not enough to study the ancient books; one has to research 'the book of nature' as well. Sturm practiced a three-step method: first, one has to describe the phenomena as accurately as possible; then catalogue the explanatory theories proposed by ancient and modern authors; and finally, extract the proper explanation from the available literature. In science, eclecticism was both 'modern' and 'elitist'.[195] When Swedenborg studied mathematics and physics in the early eighteenth century, the foremost scientists shared Sturm's basic philosophy, and the Swede made it his own. Extending far beyond natural philosophy, the spirit of eclecticism came to pervade the whole of philosophy. All true philosophy, asserted Denis Diderot (1713–1784) in the *Encyclopédie*, is eclectic in nature. '*La philosophie eclectique*' existed in antiquity, but then 'remained forgotten until the end of the sixteenth century', when it was reborn under Giordano Bruno (1548–1600), Francis Bacon (1561–1626), René Descartes (1596–1650), Thomas Hobbes (1588–1679), Gottfried Wilhelm

---

194 Michael Albrecht, *Eklektik. Eine Begriffsgeschichte*, Stuttgart 1994, pp. 307–357.
195 Albrecht, *Eklektik*, p. 330.

Leibniz (1646–1716), Nicolas de Malebranche (1638–1715), and a long list of other heroes of Diderot.[196] Among the eclectic philosophers, some would not have considered including Christian ideas in their system; others, however, were open to traditional Christian claims, accepting the notion of divine revelation, and rejecting the purely mechanistic description of nature.[197]

As befits a man of such philosophical persuasion, Swedenborg's learning was extensive as well as eclectic, his thought stemming from a wide variety of sources. In retrospect, Ralph Waldo Emerson (1803–1882) – a man well acquainted with the merits of eclecticism – could write: 'Swedenborg was born into an atmosphere of great ideas. It is hard to say what was his own.'[198] If Swedenborg's thought were to be compared to a house, it would be one in which building materials from different sources were combined to form an integrated, solid new structure. But what were these building materials and where did they come from? The following is an attempt to define some of the intellectual materials out of which Swedenborg constructed his system and to trace their historical origins. Archaic, Neoplatonic, Renaissance, baroque, and romantic elements can be discerned. The first subject will be the archaic aspect of his worldview.

An archaic worldview

Ancient peoples found themselves in a world marked by two opposite, conflicting experiences.[199] There were stability and order, manifesting themselves in the perennial cycle of day and night, birth and death. 'As long as the earth endures, seedtime and harvest, cold and heat, summer and winter, day and night, shall not cease' (Genesis 8:22). That order extended from nature to society and was also seen as valid for the realm of the spirits and deities. Divinely appointed and unchanging, this order was essentially timeless. Yet it was never wholly tranquil and stable, for there was the second, equally commonplace experience – that of instability, conflict and chaos. Drought could

---

196 Denis Diderot, *Oeuvres complètes*, Paris 1876, vol. 14, p. 345. This is Diderot's article 'Eclecticisme' for the *Encyclopédie*, 1755.
197 Ulrich Gaier, 'Nachwirkungen Oetingers in Goethes *Faust*', in: *Pietismus und Neuzeit* 10 (1984), pp. 90–123, here pp. 90–91; Horst Dreitzel, 'Zur Entwicklung und Eigenart der eklektischen Philosophie', *Zeitschrift für historische Forschung* 18 (1991), pp. 281–343, here pp. 332–333.
198 Ralph Waldo Emerson, *Representative Men* [1849], Boston 1903, p. 103.
199 Norman Cohn, *Cosmos, Chaos, and the World to Come: The Ancient Roots of Apocalyptic Faith*. 2nd ed., New Haven 2001, pp. 3–76.

upset the seasons, infertility threaten the continuity of the generations, disease and war let death reign supreme over life and prosperity. For all their disruptive power, however, the forces of chaos could never completely triumph over the divinely appointed order of creation. While the world is always liable to disturbance and full of conflict, the gods, it seemed, hold the world in timeless equilibrium between cosmos and chaos, with the balance usually tipped somewhat in the direction of cosmic order. The overall impression the world made on archaic humankind was one of visible and ultimately reliable stability, tempered by a strong sense of insecurity.

The world of the archaic peoples did not stop at the limits of everyday awareness; it extended well beyond its confines. Some form of heaven and hell – the abode of the favoured, and the less than favoured, dead – belonged to this worldview. The blissful realm is repeatedly described in the Rig-Veda, ancient Sanskrit hymns composed around 1200 BCE in India.[200] In these hymns, heaven appears as full of light, harmony, and joy. Its denizens are nourished on milk and honey. They make love – all the more delectably because they have been freed from every bodily defect. The sound of sweet singing and of the flute is readily audible. A typical hell was that of the ancient Mesopotamians: a netherworld peopled by demons who sometimes swarm out into the world of the living and even make assaults on the world of the gods. The same netherworld also housed the spirits of many dead human beings. Pictured as a realm of darkness and ruled by an unfriendly goddess, hell was a gloomy, unpleasant place.

In his dialogue *Phaedo*, the Greek philosopher Plato discusses the fate of the soul after death, assigning them places according to sinfulness or saintliness in life:

> When she [the soul] arrives at the place where the other souls are gathered, if she be impure and have done impure deeds, whether foul murders or other crimes which are the brothers of these, and the works of brothers in crime – from that soul every one flees and turns away; no one will be her companion, no one her guide, but alone she wanders in extremity of evil until certain times are fulfilled, and when they are fulfilled, she is borne irresistibly to her own fitting habitation. [...] Those who appear to be incurable by reason of the greatness of their crimes – who have committed many and terrible deeds of sacrilege, murders foul and violent, or the like – such are hurled into Tartarus which is their suitable destiny, and they never come out. [...] Those who have been pre-eminent in holiness of life are released from this earthly prison [i.e., the body], and go to their pure home which is above, and dwell in the purer earth; and of these, such as have duly purified themselves with philosophy live henceforth altogether without the body, in mansions fairer still, which may not be described, and of which the time would fail me to tell.[201]

---

200 Cohn, *Cosmos, Chaos, and the World to Come*, p. 76.
201 Plato, *Phaedo* 108 B–C; 113 E; 114 B–C.

Plato seems to have added certain ideas of his own – calling the body the soul's prison and seeing philosophy as the most powerful means of achieving a higher post-mortem status; yet, in designating a particular destination for each type of soul, his basic view agrees with archaic notions.

The Iranian prophet Zoroaster, who lived some time around 1200 BCE, revised the archaic worldview by intensifying its dramatic dimension.[202] The conflict between the forces of order and the powers of chaos was not simply everlasting; instead, it would escalate some day to a final clash of arms and armies. This war of apocalyptic dimensions would result in the victory of the creator god and final defeat, if not annihilation, to his opponents. As a result, human history would come to an end. A new world without conflict would be established. Zoroaster's worldview influenced ancient Jewish beliefs and through them Christian eschatological doctrines. The war scenario was supplemented by a judgment scenario, so that the dramatic end and consummation of human history came to be seen as consisting of two final acts – Satan's defeat and the Last Judgment.

In *De Coelo*, Swedenborg boldly brushes the Zoroastrian-Christian doctrine aside in order to revert to the archaic worldview. For him, history will continue forever as a place of conflict between good and evil, truth and falsehood, order and disorder. He offers a radical new interpretation of traditional Christian teachings on the Last Judgment, arguing that the relevant biblical texts have been misunderstood (nos. 1, 307, 312). He claims to have been granted the discovery of the real meaning concealed in the Bible. From *De Coleo* alone, although it is not directly discussed, one can infer that for Swedenborg the Last Judgment has already taken place as an event not on earth, but in the spiritual world. In *De Ultimo Judicio, et de Babylonia destructa* (The Last Judgment and Babylon Destroyed, 1758, no. 45) he describes it as an event he had himself witnessed in 1757. *De Coelo* includes a brief description:

> I have seen mountains that were the abode of evil people levelled and overturned, sometimes shaken from end to end as happens in our earthquakes. I have seen cliffs split down the middle right to the bottom and the evil people on them swallowed up. I have also seen angels scatter some hundreds of thousands of evil spirits and cast them into hell. (no. 229)

Although this report is accompanied by a reference to *De Ultimo Judicio*, which describes the Last Judgment in detail, uninformed readers would hardly suspect that the author is speaking here about the Last Judgment as a past event, an episode contemporaneous with human history rather than its culmination that

---

202 Mary Boyce, *A History of Zoroastrianism*, Leiden 1975, vol. 1, p. 190 dates Zoroaster between 1400 and 1000 BCE.

brings this history to a close. Swedenborg chose to devote a separate book – *De Ultimo Judicio* – to this important subject.

According to the Christian Creed, Christ 'will come again in glory to judge the living and the dead, and his kingdom will have no end'.[203] This article of faith is generally understood in apocalyptic terms as a reference to a great cosmic drama that marks the end of human history. In modern theology, belief in the 'end of the world' has become quite controversial, and many theologians are looking for a meaning beyond the mere words. For them, eschatological scenarios described in the New Testament and summarised in the creed are not meant as predictions of, and explanations of, future events. Instead, they must have some symbolic meaning, to be recovered by special strategies of interpretation.

Three of these strategies have become quite common among theologians. One school sees the New Testament apocalyptic drama as a secondary, post-Jesuanic level of early-Christian tradition. On this premise Jesus' ministry can be understood within the archaic worldview. Seen from this perspective, his healings appear as temporary victories in the battle against the forces of evil, aiming at the establishment of God's sovereign rule over people. Even though Jesus may have wished to cure Jewish society as a whole, he never went beyond hoping for an immediate, though temporary, triumph over the forces of evil. Jesus' re-establishment of divine rulership is small-scale and realistic and forms but one episode of the struggle between order and chaos. There is no need to make it a minor prelude to an apocalyptic event of universal dimensions. The historical Jesus, as some modern historians see him, never gave his message a utopian and apocalyptic frame.[204]

A second strategy for revising traditional Christian eschatological beliefs can be seen in the work of the Catholic theologian Gerhard Lohfink. According to him there will be an individual judgment only after each person's death; as a cosmic drama, the Last Judgment will never take place, and this may be understood as the result of the fact that from God's timeless perspective, all individual judgments happen at the same time.[205]

The third relevant strategy, represented by the Lutheran theologian Rudolf Bultmann, considers that the mythological eschatology must have an existential message. Rather than being a literal announcement of the Last Judgment, it

---

203 From the Constantinopolitan Creed of 381 CE. See John H. Leith (ed.), *Creeds of the Churches*. Revised edition, Richmond 1973, p. 33.
204 Bernhard Lang, *Sacred Games: A History of Christian Worship*, New Haven 1997, pp. 94–96.
205 Gerhard Lohfink, 'Zur Möglichkeit christlicher Naherwartung', in: Gisbert Greshake and Gerhard Lohfink, *Naherwartung – Auferstehung – Unsterblichkeit*, Freiburg 1975, pp. 38–81, here pp. 70–81.

serves as an urgent summons to confront God here and now and find our authentic inner being. When people discover God as the ultimate reality, then everything else – the material world and its history – vanishes. This is how Bultmann explains the real, inner meaning of the biblical message of the 'end of the world':

> Eschatological preaching views the present time in the light of the future and it says that this present world of nature and history, the world in which we live our lives and make our plans is not the only world; that this world is temporal and transitory, yes, ultimately empty and unreal in the face of eternity.[206]

Like Swedenborg, much of modern theology eliminates apocalyptic scenarios and returns to archaic views of the perennial struggle between alienating and liberating, divine and demonic forces. Swedenborg's Last Judgment is unique, however, inasmuch as he describes it as a single significant event that has already taken place.

Neoplatonic features

One of the very first things we are told in *De Coelo* is that 'the Divine is one' (*quod Divinum unum sit*, no. 2). This One (*unum*) is the 'First' (*Primum*), and whatever exists both in this world and in the other realms of the universe owes its existence to the One. We must not think of existing beings – both material and immaterial, animate and inanimate, animal and human – as self-sufficient. Rather, their being has to be constantly replenished from the First, the source of all being. Everything depends on the First for strength and vitality. 'If anything were not kept in constant connection with the First, through intermediate means, it would instantly collapse and disintegrate' (no. 9). Nothing stands on its own as a complete and independent substance; everything derives its power of being from a transcendent, otherworldly source – from the One or the First.

These statements form the elementary ontological lesson not only of Swedenborg, but of a long and venerable philosophical tradition begun in ancient Greece by Plato in the fourth century BCE, and renewed as well as developed by Plotinus (205–270) in the third century CE.[207]

Platonic philosophy teaches three main doctrines. First, that there are two worlds – a material one and a spiritual, transcendent one, with the spiritual world

---

206 Rudolf Bultmann, *Jesus Christ and Mythology*, New York 1958, p. 23.
207 For an introductory summary of the philosophy of Plotinus and the impact it made in Western intellectual life, see R. Baine Harris, 'A Brief Description of Neoplatonism', in: idem (ed.), *The Significance of Neoplatonism*, Albany, N.Y. 1976, pp. 1–20.

being the purer and more powerful realm. Second, that both worlds are ultimately derived from a common source of being and power that transcends everything spiritual and material. This source can be spoken of as the Good, the One, the First, or the deity. Third, the human being belongs essentially to the spiritual or divine world and therefore transcends death; the general way of referring to this doctrine is to say that the individual human soul is immortal.

Stated in these very general terms, much if not all of Christian theology parallels Platonic or Neoplatonic thought. However, Swedenborg sometimes uses the very terminology employed by the school of Plato – for example, when calling God 'the First'. According to one of Plato's most important doctrines, everything that exists derives its being from an ultimately transcendent source, and it must stay in contact with that source in order not to fall into nothingness. God or the Good, in Plato as in Swedenborg symbolised by the sun, brings entities 'into existence and gives them growth and nourishment'; they 'derive from the Good [...] their very being and reality'.[208] Swedenborg also uses specifically Neoplatonic ideas and teachings. The statement already quoted above is a perfect example: 'If anything were not kept in constant connection with the First, through intermediate means (*in nexu continue tenetur per intermedia cum Primo*), it would instantly collapse and disintegrate' (no. 9). The First, in Platonic thought, is transcendent and very remote from most spiritual and material realities, so that there must be an *intermedium*, or intermediary, that connects all beings with their ultimate source. 'Anything existing after the First must necessarily arise from that First, whether immediately or via intermediaries', states Plotinus.[209] Platonists have spent much time trying to define this *intermedium*; Plotinus, for instance, developed the theory of a cosmic soul that binds all things together, connecting them with the One or the First. In Swedenborg, angels fulfil the *intermedium* function: 'We cannot move a step without the inflow (*influxus*) of heaven', he observes. He adds that 'angels have been allowed to activate my walking, my actions, my tongue and my conversation as they wished, by flowing into my intention and thinking' (no. 228). In one passage, Plotinus also refers to divine guidance by way of inflow: 'Once the soul receives an outflow [emanation] coming to her from the Good, she is excited and seized with Bacchic madness, and filled with stinging desires: thus love is born. [...] Once, however, a warmth from the Good has reached her, she is strengthened and awakened.'[210] The 'outflow' (from the Divine) and 'inflow' (into the soul) that in Plotinus excites the soul to love is in

---

208 Plato, *Republic* VI, 509 B.
209 Plotinus, *Enneads* V, 4,1.
210 Plotinus, *Enneads* VI, 7,22.

Swedenborg generalised to all impulses of human will and human thought. All forms of love – marital love (*amor conjugialis*) as well as simpler forms of mutual love (*amor mutuus*) – also derive from heavenly inflow. 'Marital love comes down from the Lord through heaven' – *Amor conjugialis a Domino per Coelum descendat* (no. 385).

Plotinus and Swedenborg share one conspicuous stylistic feature in their writing and developing an argument: the alternation of conceptual discussion with vivid description of spiritual experiences. When writing in an abstract manner about good and truth and their emanation from the Lord and their inflow into human beings, they rarely fail to conclude the discussion by illustrating the argument from 'things heard and seen' in the spiritual world. The two philosophers are matched in their endeavour to exhaust the resources of language and communication to make their point. Hence Plotinus's

> tendency to conclude passages of arid dialectical discussion with one of his vivid descriptions of contemplation or of mystical experience, and his stress that only in the light of such experiences can all difficulties be resolved. Also relevant in this context is Plotinus' use of imagery, especially of the so-called 'dynamic images', in which processes drawn from the material world are used to illustrate the activity of the spiritual order.[211]

The following parables, illustrating the divine presence in the world, can give an idea of Plotinus's charming use of metaphor and imagery:

> The Soul [of the cosmos] watches the ceaselessly changing universe and follows all the fate of all its works: this is its life, and it knows no respite from its care, but is ever labouring to bring about perfection, planning to lead all to an unending state of excellence – like a farmer, first sowing and planting and then constantly setting to rights where rainstorms and long frosts and high gales have played havoc.[212]
>
> Imagine that a stately and complex mansion house has been built. Its architect has never abandoned it, yet he is not tied down to it. He has judged it worthy in all its length and breadth of all the care that can serve to its being – as far as it can share in being – or to its beauty, but this care is without burden to its director, who never descends, but presides over it from above: this shows the degree to which the cosmos is ensouled – not by a soul that belongs to it, but by one present to it; it is mastered, not master; not possessor but possessed. The soul bears it up, and it lies within, no fragment of it left in isolation.[213]

The cosmic soul, for Plotinus, is an emanation from the One that, by being present in everything, connects everything with the One as its ultimate, divine source of being. One final example, the symbolic use of the human body, can serve to illustrate how Plotinian language can be very close to that of Swedenborg. The author of *De Coelo* often uses the human body as an

---

211 R. T. Wallis, *Neoplatonism*, London 1972, p. 41.
212 Plotinus, *Enneads* II, 3,16.
213 Plotinus, *Enneads* IV, 3,9.

illuminating analogy in his arguments. Thus he asserts that the universe as a whole is in human form and that the highest or third heaven corresponds to the head of the Grand Man or Universal Human (no. 65). In the school of Plato we find similar ideas. Consider the following passage from Plotinus:

> In every living being the upper parts – head, face – are the most beautiful, the mid and lower members inferior. In the Universe the middle and lower members are human beings; above them, the Heavens and the gods that dwell there. These gods with the entire circling expanse of the heavens constitute the greater part of the cosmos.[214]

If we substitute the angels for Plotinus's gods, then we have a statement that comes close to what Swedenborg might have written. Thus many of Swedenborg's ideas echo both the thought and the language of Europe's oldest and most venerable philosophy. This being said, one major difference between *De Coelo* and the Neoplatonic view of God must be pointed out. In classical Neoplatonism the First or One stays remote from creation and is difficult to reach even by philosophical meditation. Swedenborg's Christian Neoplatonism insists that the One is the Lord, that is, Jesus Christ who manifested himself within the realm of the inhabited world and therefore can be thought about, believed in, and loved. (Interestingly, Swedenborg does not offer a critique of Neoplatonism. His critique of those who speak about a deity which is somehow identical with nature but cannot be grasped by human thought or love, found in no. 3, seems to be directed against Neostoic philosophy.)

Not only the *Enneads* of Plotinus himself, but also other Neoplatonic works can be compared fruitfully with *De Coelo*. Here the most prominent source is the *Corpus Hermeticum*, a series of religious and philosophical treatises dating from the second and third centuries. According to one of the books included in this corpus and reminiscent of Swedenborg – *Hermes Trismegistos*, libellus XVI –, two powers compete for dominion over each human soul. One of these powers is represented by the host of demons, evil spirits that

> mould our souls into another shape, and pull them away to themselves, being seated in our nerves [or sinews] and marrow and veins and arteries, and penetrating even to our inmost organs. [...] These demons then make their way through the body, and enter into the two irrational parts of the soul; and each demon perverts the soul in a different way, according to his special mode of action.[215]

There is a third, rational part of the soul, however, and this part remains immune to demonic assaults:

---

214 Plotinus, *Enneads* III, 2,8.
215 *Hermes Trismegistos* XVI, 14–15 (Walter Scott, editor and translator, *Hermetica*, vol. 1, Oxford 1924, p. 271).

Free from dominion by the demons, the rational part of the human soul is fit to receive God into itself. If then the rational part of the human soul is illumined by a ray of light from God, for that human being the working of the demons is brought to naught, for no demon and no god has power against a single ray of the light of God. But such humans are few indeed.[216]

True to its Neoplatonic elitism, the *Corpus Hermeticum* argues that only a few people have been touched by the divine light.

Neoplatonic philosophy intrigued and inspired Christian thinkers in antiquity, including Origen (ca. 185–254), Augustine (354–430), and Pseudo-Dionysius (ca. 500). The Italian philosopher Marsilio Ficino (1433–1499), enamoured by the thinking of Plotinus, translated this author's Greek works into Latin, making them accessible to European readers. Ficino also produced a Latin version of the *Corpus Hermeticum*, then thought to belong to the world's most ancient literature – a literature predating the biblical books written by Moses. In the seventeenth century the so-called Cambridge Platonists, a school represented by Henry More (1614–1687) and Ralph Cudworth (1617–1688), reinvigorated Platonic thought, defending it against those scientists who adopted a mechanistic worldview. Among earlier researchers, Martin Lamm emphasised Swedenborg's closeness to if not indebtedness to Neoplatonic philosophy.[217] The author of *De Coelo* mentions Plotinus by name only once, in a quotation from Augustine,[218] but he seems to have known Plotinus' works in Ficino's translation. The Diocesan Library of Linköping in Sweden owns a Latin copy of Plotinus's works (published in Basel 1580) that Swedenborg had signed with his name in 1705.[219] So at one point in his long intellectual career he must have become acquainted with Neoplatonic thought, and it may have inspired him to construct his own thinking along similar lines. Among Swedenborg's known philosophical authorities, Leibniz is perhaps closest to Neoplatonism;[220] see for instance his assertion that 'the creature depends continually upon divine operation, and that it depends upon that no less after the time of its beginning than when it first begins. This dependence implies that it would not continue to exist if God did not continue to act'.[221] On this important point, Plotinus, Leibniz, and Swedenborg all agree.

---

216 *Hermes Trismegistos*, XVI, 15–16 (Scott, ed., *Hermetica*, vol. 1, p. 271).
217 Lamm, *Swedenborg*.
218 Emanuel Swedenborg, *A Philosopher's Note Book*. Translated by A. Acton, Philadelphia 1931, p. 131.
219 Lamm, *Swedenborg*, p. 62.
220 Kurt P. Nemitz, 'Leibniz and Swedenborg', *The New Philosophy* 94 (1991), pp. 445–488; idem, 'The German Philosophers Leibniz and Wolff in Swedenborg's Philosophic Development', *The New Philosophy* 97 (1994), pp. 411–425.
221 Gottfried Wilhelm Leibniz, Theodicy [1710]. Translated by A. Farrar, New Haven, 1952, p. 355, in agreement with Swedenborg, *De Coelo* no. 385.

During the seventeenth and eighteenth centuries, European intellectuals strove to develop what we now call science but which was then called natural philosophy. Certain baroque authors – nowadays called Enlightenment scientists – rejected the notion of an animated nature, based their ideas exclusively on verifiable experience, and adopted a mechanistic worldview.[222] By contrast others, like George Berkeley (1685–1753), stayed closer to Neoplatonic traditions, upon which they drew, and made them key elements of their *'philosophia eclectica'*.[223] Although always religious, Swedenborg had adopted a mechanistic worldview in his early, philosophical works. Ultimately he found it wanting and came to prefer a more Neoplatonic perspective.

Renaissance ideas and ideals

Both Plotinus and Emanuel Swedenborg remained unmarried, did not care much about eating,[224] and spent all their lives in intellectual pursuits. They also shared basic philosophical ideas about the divine. However, not all of Swedenborg's teachings echo Neoplatonic ideas. In certain respects, the author of *De Coelo* was quite different from Plotinus. Their attitude toward wealth and wordly occupations differed considerably.

The ancient philosopher praised one of his friends, the Roman Senator Rogatianus, holding him up as a model to those aiming at leading a philosophical life. Rogatianus, according to Porphyry's *Life of Plotinus*, had 'advanced to such detachment from political ambitions that he gave up all his property, dismissed all his slaves, renounced every dignity. [...] He even abandoned his own house, spending his time here and there at his friends' and acquaintances', sleeping and eating with them and taking, at that, only one meal every other day'.[225] Plotinus recommended a life of poverty and world-renouncement, preferring

---

222 Sigmund Bonk, *Abschied von der Anima mundi. Die britische Philosophie im Vorfeld der industriellen Revolution*, Freiburg 1999.
223 Sladek 1984, p. 145.
224 Porphyry, *Life of Plotinus* 8: 'Even his sleep was kept light by abstemiousness that often prevented him taking as much as a piece of bread.' – In his diary, Swedenborg notes under April 1745: 'At mid-day, about dinner time, an angel who was with me spoke to me, saying that I was not to indulge the belly too much at the table' (Swedenborg, *Spiritual Diary*, London 1889, vol. 1, no. 329). In the years following this angelic advice, Swedenborg apparently did not eat much (Tafel, *Documents*, vol. 2/3, pp. 537, 544; Johann Christian Cuno, *Memoirs on Swedenborg*, Bryn Athyn, Penn. 1947, p. 11), often living on a simple diet of almonds and raisins (Tafel, *Documents*, vol. 2/3, p. 540).
225 Porphyry, *On the Life of Plotinus* 7.

contemplation and meditation to the active life in the world. In its Augustinian form, Neoplatonic philosophy suited Christian ascetics and world-renouncers and could be invoked by medieval monks. Swedenborg would have none of this. Only ignorant people prefer an existence characterised by 'spurning worldly interests, especially concerns for money and prestige, going around in constant meditation about God, salvation, and eternal life, devoting their lives to prayer and reading the Word [that is, the Bible] and religious literature'. No, says Swedenborg, 'if we would accept the life of heaven, we need by all means to live in the world and to participate in its duties and affairs' (no. 528). Ultimately based on selfishness and a high degree of self-love – as opposed to being unselfish and of use to the community –, mortification makes life mournful and gloomy; it prepares for hell rather than for sainthood in heaven (nos. 528, 535).

What Swedenborg says of the life of worldly duties also applies to wealth: it does not stand in the way of spiritual authenticity.

> It is all right to acquire wealth and accumulate any number of assets, as long as it is not done by fraud or evil devices. It is all right to eat and drink elegantly, as long as we do not invest our lives in such things. It is all right to be housed as graciously as befits one's station, to chat with others like us, to go to games, to consult about worldly affairs. [...] There is no need to give to the poor except as the spirit moves us. (no. 358)

In other words: Swedenborg tells no one to sell his or her property and lead a different life. He would not have approved of Plotinus's friend, the Roman Senator Rogatianus. To him, Rogatianus must have appeared a strange man. Swedenborg would have told him that what ultimately counts is not the outward behaviour but the inner state, for 'our quality is that of our affection and thought, or our love and faith' (*homo enim talis est qualis ejus affectio & cogitatio*, no. 358).

In his negative attitude to world-renouncement and in his appreciation of the trappings of wealth, the author of *De Coelo* departs from the Neoplatonic and medieval Catholic traditions. His values are those of the Renaissance. While the medieval attitude continued to be visible in the eighteenth century, the Renaissance with its new cultural, intellectual, political, and religious style had penetrated all of Europe, including Sweden and Britain. Scholars and merchants, poets and prelates considered life 'in the world' to be at least as pure and worthy as that of the monk's retreat. Rather than renouncing the world, they said, we should shape and enjoy it. Renaissance theology insisted that as noble beings we are invited to enjoy rather than renounce the world. The first chapter of the book of Genesis sanctioned the ideal of an active life, detailing how creative humankind reflects the image of God the Creator. By loving, enjoying, and participating in God's world, Christians display their love of God.[226] In the early sixteenth century, Rodrigo Borgia (1431–1503; alias Pope Alexander VI), Erasmus of Rotterdam (1466–1536), Machiavelli (1469–1527), and Michelangelo (1475–1564) symbolized the Renaissance interest in art and architecture, books and building, wealth, women, and worldly power. In the eighteenth century, the very same interests still fascinated the intellectual and cultural elite, and Swedenborg's dictum 'without an active life, there is no happiness' (*absque vita activa, nulla vitae felicitas,* no. 403) can easily pass for a Renaissance maxim. There would be no Gottfried Wilhelm Leibniz and Immanuel Kant (1724–1804) in Germany, no Voltaire (1694–1778) in France, no Isaac Newton (1642–1747) in England, no Emanuel Swedenborg in Sweden if the Renaissance had not prepared their way.

Lorenzo Valla (1405–1457), one of the most important Renaissance authors, broke with many medieval Catholic ideas. In *The Profession of the Religious* he denied that institutionalized monastic virtue had superior validity, and asserted that spontaneous good actions were higher.[227] Swedenborg's critical attitude toward monasticism and his preference for 'giving to the poor as the spirit moves us' (no. 358) speak the same language and reflect the same Renaissance atmosphere of thought.

As has been demonstrated, the Renaissance appreciation of wealth and worldliness rests on a firm theological basis: the insight into the goodness of creation. It also rests on a philosophical foundation – the idea of human freedom and self-determination. Unlike animals, human beings can determine their fate free from the constraints of inborn dispositions. A few lines from Giovanni Pico della Mirandola's famous *Oratio de hominis dignitate* (1486, Oration on Human Dignity) can serve as a condensed statement of the intellectual atmosphere within which Swedenborg thought. Pico puts the following words in the mouth of God as he speaks to Adam in Paradise:

> Neither a fixed abode nor a form that is yours alone nor any function peculiar to yourself have we given you, Adam, to the end that according to your longing and according to your judgment you may have and possess what abode, what form, and what functions you yourself shall desire. The nature of all other beings is limited and constrained within the bounds of laws prescribed by us. You, constrained by no limits, in accordance with your own free will, in whose hand we have placed you, shall ordain for yourself the limits of your nature. We have set you at the world's centre that you may from thence more easily observe whatever is in the world. We have made you neither of heaven nor of earth, neither mortal nor immortal,

---

226 Charles Trinkaus, *In Our Image and Likeness: Humanity and Divinity in Italian Humanist Thought*, Chicago 1970.
227 Charles Trinkaus, in: Ernst Cassirer et al. (eds.), *The Renaissance Philosophy of Man*, Chicago 1948, p. 151.

so that with freedom of choice and with honour, as though the maker and moulder of yourself, you may fashion yourself in whatever shape you shall prefer. You shall have the power to degenerate into the lower forms of life, which are brutish. You shall have the power, out of your soul's judgment, to be reborn into the higher forms, which are divine.[228]

With but little adjustment these could be the very words of Swedenborg.

Freedom, for Renaissance philosophers and for Swedenborg, has to do with the human faculty of will or volition. In this context, as in many others, the author of *De Coelo* focuses on the distinction between volition and intellect as our basic mental capacities (nos. 423–425, 500). The vocabulary he uses can be presented as follows:

essential mental capacities:	will/volition/intention (*voluntas*)	intellect/understanding (*intellectus, cogitatio*)
mental states:	love (*amor*)	wisdom (*sapientia*)
extra-mental realities:	good (*bonum*) or evil (*malum*)	truth (*verum*) or falsehood (*falsum*)

Table 5.3 Swedenborg's distinction between will and intellect

If the human being is to be free, it must have a free will. Before Pico, Augustine had asserted this fact in *De libero arbitrio* (On Free Will, dating from 388/395); after him, the prince of humanists, Erasmus of Rotterdam, did so in a work of the same title—*De libero arbitrio* (On Free Will, 1524). Here we have to remember that in the Renaissance philosophical discussion supported the idea that the action-oriented human will, rather than the contemplation-oriented intellect, was the noblest human faculty.[229] While medieval scholastics invoked the authority of Aristotle to defend their contemplative ideals, Renaissance writers preferred Cicero (106–43 BCE), the active statesman and orator, the man of resolve. This Renaissance tradition reached Swedenborg through authors such as Malebranche (died 1715), Leibniz (died 1715), and Christian Wolff (died 1754).[230] According to Swedenborg, the human faculty of volition (*voluntas*) also ranks above the intellect or cognitive ability. Priority is given to the human will

---

228 Pico della Mirandola, *De hominis dignitate* 3 (Ernst Cassirer et al., eds., *The Renaissance Philosophy of Man*, Chicago 1948, pp. 224–225. I have adapted the translation of E. L. Forbes).
229 Trinkaus, *In Our Image and Likeness*, p. 73.
230 See Swedenborg, *A Philosopher's Note Book*, pp. 54–59 for Swedenborg's excerpts on the notion of the will. Nemitz comments on the influence of Leibniz and Wolff on Swedenborg (see above, note 40).

and, consequently, to everything that is on the left side of table 5.3 – volition, love, good. 'Our volition', he states, 'is the substance of our life [...], while our cognitive ability is the consequent manifestation of life' (no. 26, note i). In the spiritual world, the highest heaven – the one called the heavenly kingdom – is defined as 'the voluntary part of heaven' (no. 95). In more philosophical terms, 'thought is nothing but the form of our intention' (*cogitatio non aliud est quam voluntatis forma*, no. 500). In the ordering of the faculties of the human mind, then, volition holds the highest rank. For the author of *De Coelo* it follows that 'nothing is ever free unless it comes from our volition' (no. 598,2).

But how can a human being be free? Swedenborg describes the environment in which humans live as one where good and evil influences blend: 'By means of the spirits from hell we encounter our evil, and by means of the angels from heaven we encounter the good we have from the Lord. As a result, we are in a spiritual equilibrium – that is, in freedom' (no. 599). It is in freedom that humans can decide whether to associate with heaven or hell and thus determine their ultimate destiny. As the only free beings in the universe, men and women stand at the centre of the cosmos. It is up to them whether they open themselves to the inflowing of good and truth from the Lord, or not. Thus both heaven and hell are peopled with free beings. The Renaissance idea of human freedom has never been asserted more consistently.

All human beings enjoy this freedom, not just Christians. Therefore all human beings can live a moral life in which they attach themselves to the good and to the Lord. And therefore all can attain heavenly existence. While traditional Christian theology was prepared to relegate pagans to hell (as did Dante in his *Inferno*), Swedenborg recognises their capacity to enter heaven (nos. 318–328). In so doing he has famous Renaissance humanists on his side: Erasmus of Rotterdam and the Swiss reformer Ulrich Zwingli (1484–1531). For Erasmus, one does not have to be a Christian to become a saint; and Christians may even rely on pagan intercession in heaven; so why not pray, '*Sancte Socrates, ora pro nobis*' – Saint Socrates, pray for us?[231] Unlike the other, less liberal reformers, Zwingli also admitted pagans to heaven. Hoping to lure the French king François I to the Protestant cause, Zwingli promised him eternal felicity in the company of his own pious ancestors as well as biblical figures. With a splendid humanist flourish he added that characters like Hercules, Socrates, the Catos, and the Scipios would also await the king in heaven.[232] Together with Jesus, Socrates

---

231 Erasmus, 'The Godly Feast' [*Convivium religiosum*, 1552], in: idem, *Collected Works*. Translated by C.R. Thompson, Toronto 1997, vol. 39, p. 194.
232 Ulrich Zwingli, 'Exposition of the Faith' [1531], in *Zwingli and Bullinger*. Edited by G.W. Bromiley, London 1953, pp. 275–276. See W. Peter Stephens, 'Zwingli and the Salvation

formed the moral paradigm of the Renaissance, and so it would not have made sense to exclude him from heaven. If all are free to lead a truly moral and spiritual life, then heaven is open to all.

The enjoyment of wealth and universal self-determination form part of what Renaissance philosophers have termed the dignity of the human being. But although wealth and freedom are important aspects of this dignity, they are in some ways secondary. Swedenborg digs deeper, insisting that there must be more to human dignity. He argued that in the human being there is a spark of the divine or an inner point of contact with the Deity that is the foundation of one's dignity. From his hesitant language we can see that Swedenborg found it difficult to express himself on this point; yet, his meaning is clear enough. Within every human being there is 'a central and highest something (*intimum & supremum quoddam*), where the Lord's divine life flows in first and most intimately.' It is this 'central or highest level that makes us human and distinguishes us from the lower animals, since they do not have it. This is why we, unlike animals, can be raised up by the Lord toward himself. [...] It is also why we live forever' (no. 39). The divine indwelling in the human person is beyond human perception or, in other words, it belongs to the basic ontological structure. It is this 'central and highest something' that makes us the central and highest something within the universe. It makes us the only intelligent and responsive partners of the Lord himself.

The Lord's partners, according to some Renaissance thinkers, do not have to originate on the planet earth. In the fifteenth century the cardinal Nicholas of Cusa (1401–1464) in *Of Learned Ignorance* (1440) supported the idea of a plurality of inhabited worlds and the existence of life on the moon and sun. The most interesting Renaissance statement comes from the Franciscan theologian Guillaume de Vaurouillon (1392–1463), who taught in Paris. While he did not believe in the existence of worlds other than our own, he argued that it would not be difficult for God to create them. 'Infinite worlds, more perfect than this one, lie hid in the mind of God. [...] It is possible that the species of each of these worlds is distinguished from those of our world.'[233] Vaurouillon did not envisage knowledge of those worlds, far-off and separate, coming to earth except through angelic communication or some other special divine means. Soon, the idea was to receive support from both traditional and scientific cosmology. In 1473 the recently discovered book *De rerum natura*, written in the first century BCE by

---

of the Gentiles', in: idem (ed.), *The Bible, the Reformation and the Church*, Sheffield 1995, pp. 224–244.

233 Guillaume de Vaurouillon, quoted by Thomas F. O'Meara, 'Christian Theology and Extraterrestrial Intelligent Life', *Theological Studies* 60 (1999), pp. 1–30, here p. 15.

the Epicurean philosopher Lucretius (ca. 96–55 BCE), became available in print; this book's pluralist teaching acquainted European intellectuals with the idea. In the sixteenth century, scientific support came from Nicolaus Copernicus (1473–1543), whose heliocentric redescription of the universe made the earth one planet among other, possibly inhabited, planets. By the eighteenth century, the idea of an inhabited universe had become commonplace and was shared by most philosophers and scientists,[234] including Swedenborg.[235] When in 1757 Pope Benedict XIV (1675–1758) lifted the ban on works expounding heliocentrism,[236] the story of the medieval cosmos ended, and a new story could begin – that of an infinite universe with a plurality of worlds.

The other life in baroque thought

Biographies of Emanuel Swedenborg regularly include a plate showing one of the few portraits that exist of him: a man with erect and vigorous physique, big smiling eyes, wearing a white, curly, powdered wig, a dress-coat of black velvet, and a white shirt with frilled sleeves: a man easily recognised as a modestly attired aristocrat of the baroque age. The portrait reminds us of the fact that the author of *De Coelo*, while thoroughly familiar with the traditions of the past, was also a man of his own century and his own culture. The baroque age of the seventeenth and eighteenth centuries boasted a rich artistic, literary, religious, and political culture, of which the terms Enlightenment (that is, baroque rationalism) and 'classical music' can capture no more than small fragments. One particular feature of the baroque mind, which no one can miss, is its almost excessive attention to and interest in detail: in map making, travel reports, painting, architecture, historiography, biography, diary writing, novels, and theology, or any of the other subjects of its fascination. Authors, artists, and scientists strove to satisfy the hunger for well-chronicled, detailed, precise knowledge, both of the visible world of the present and the invisible realms of the past; both of far-away places and the transcendent world. None other than Goethe noted the rule: 'Only by means of the most precise detail, and infinite

---

234 Michael J. Crowe, 'A History of the Extraterrestrial Life Debate', *Zygon* 32 (1997), pp. 147–162, here p. 152.
235 Swedenborg, *De Coelo* no. 417, and his work *De Telluribus in mundo nostro solari, quae vocantur planetae* throughout.
236 W.G.L. Randles, *The Unmaking of the Medieval Christian Cosmos, 1500–1760*, Aldershot 1999, p. 217.

particulars, all vividly characteristic of the whole' can one hope to grasp a piece of reality.[237]

While relevant examples of excessive attention to elaboration and detail in travel reports, diaries and novels can be relegated to the notes,[238] this mode of presentation in cartography, art, historiography, and theology deserves at least a brief commentary here.

In 1492, Christopher Columbus discovered the continent that came to be known as America. During the following two centuries, explorers travelled throughout the world, often in the service of European royalty. Their aim was to win new islands, new wealth, and indeed new treasures for their masters and for themselves. Typically, the reports of these expeditions were considered state secrets and therefore remained unpublished. Since the way to the 'treasure islands' was to remain secret, cartographers received little information that they could use in improving their maps.[239] This attitude of secrecy changed around 1700, when a new era of exploration began. Eighteenth-century explorers such as the Dane Vitus Bering (1681–1741), the German Carsten Niebuhr (1733–1815), and the Englishman Captain James Cook (1728–1779) sought knowledge, not treasures, and therefore took great care to have their discoveries chronicled in the form of detailed reports and ever more precise maps. They linked their maps to astronomically determined coordinates that had been established by French cartographers in the late seventeenth century.[240] Around 1700, Europeans knew about 60.6 per cent of the surface of the earth; by 1800, they knew 82.6 per cent.[241] By the end of the eighteenth century, cartographers could produce fairly reliable maps of most parts of the world, and these maps look very much like those we use today.

---

237 Johann Wolfgang Goethe, *From My Life: Poetry and Truth*. Translated by R.R. Heitner, in: idem, *Collected Works*, New York 1987, vol. 4, p. 176 (book 6).

238 Mention may be made of Georg Forster (1754–1794), who chronicled one of Captain Cook's maritime voyages (*A Voyage round the World*, 1777) and Carsten Niebuhr (1733–1815), who explored and described Arabia and the adjacent countries (*Beschreibung von Arabien*, 1772). Typical baroque diaries include those of the Englishmen Samuel Pepys (1633–1703) and James Boswell (1740–1795). Swedenborg's short journal of dreams and his long diary of spiritual experiences also belong here. The English novel is essentially an eighteenth-century product; unsurpassed in descriptive detail is Laurence Sterne's *Tristram Shandy* (1760–1767) in which the author reaches the third volume before he gets around to having his hero born.

239 Arnold Scheuerbrandt, 'Die Entdeckungs- und Forschungsreisen bis zum Beginn des 19. Jahrhunderts', in: Gerhard Römer (ed.), *Imago mundi moderna. Weltkarten des Zweiten Entdeckungszeitalters*, Karlsruhe 1993, pp. 20–59, here p. 38.

240 Heinz Musall, 'Weltkarten vom Ende des 17. bis zur Mitte des 19. Jahrhunderts', in: Römer (ed.), *Imago mundi moderna*, pp. 61–72, here pp. 66–67.

241 Scheuerbrandt, 'Die Entdeckungs- und Forschungsreisen', p. 41.

Baroque artists, as exemplified by the Dutch painters, left us a full, realistic, and almost photographic record of their world. Painters were expected to give scenes of the past – historic battles, personalities, and encounters of great men – the same realistic touch in the hopes of evoking patriotic or religious feelings. In the eighteenth century, the painting of historical scenes could be considered the highest, most noble kind of art. 'He that Paints a History well', wrote Jonathan Richardson (1665–1745) in 1725, 'must be able to write it; he must be thoroughly inform'd of all things relating to it, and conceive it clearly, and nobly in his mind, or he can never express it upon the Canvas: He must have a solid Judgment, with a lively Imagination, and know what Figures, and what Incidents ought to be brought in, and what every one should Say, and Think. A painter therefore of this Class must possess all the good Qualities requisite to an Historian.'[242] The appreciation of history painting reflects the wish of the baroque age to visualise everything in the round, and in as much detail as possible.

The eighteenth century saw the first development of modern historiography – Voltaire composed his *Essai sur les moeurs et l'esprit des nations*, David Hume (1711–1776) his *History of England*, and Edward Gibbon (1737–1794) the famous *History of the Decline and Fall of the Roman Empire*, works that still rank among the classics of historical narrative. A greater wealth of petty detail could of course be included in biographies (not to mention private, then unpublished diaries), of which *The Life of Samuel Johnson*, by James Boswell (1740–1795) remains the foremost example. People read these works with admiration and regarded the historian's craft with awe. Historians were expected to recreate the past in vivid detail, to make us almost feel present at the great moments, and to grant us glimpses of domestic and everyday life. But historiography did not aim at the mere accumulation of events, names, and descriptions. It aimed at giving a coherent picture and explaining the course of history: why did the Roman Empire decline (Gibbon)? What motivated the English monarchs to act as they did? What are the limits of institutional power (Hume)? How is history shaped by religion, economy, trade, and the various customs and worldviews (Voltaire)? Far from identifying history with the mere listing of dynasties and chronicling of battles, historians considered their task as eminently philosophical and moral. Swedenborg was not a historian; but was he not a kindred spirit, striving as he did to describe the other world in vivid detail, while at the same time explaining the innermost dispositions of people, and God's dealing with them? When an early German defender of Swedenborg

---

242 Jonathan Richardson, 'An Essay on the Theory of Painting' [1725], in: Thomas W. Gathgens et al. (eds.), *Historienmalerei*, Berlin 1996, pp. 215–217, here p. 215.

strove to characterize the seer, he compared him to a historian: 'Whenever he [Swedenborg] refers to the revelatory states that he claims to have been in, he appears as someone who, with the spirit of a historiographer, observes with clear perception and narrates very truthfully and precisely.'[243]

As an integral part of culture in the seventeenth and eighteenth centuries, religion shared the general craving for detail, specificity, and precision. Catholic moral casuistry described and defined sinful acts and their circumstances in hair-splitting detail. Vying with each other in elaborate moral descriptions and 'pictures of manners', preachers of all churches inflicted long sermons on their congregations, often both on Sunday morning and afternoon (to the well-known displeasure of Swedenborg). Baroque religiosity can be measured by the intensity of its desire to imagine scenes of the Bible, of the lives of the saints, and of the heavenly world. Theologians, visionaries, and poets all strove to write in as much detail about the other world as history-painters made an effort to put it on canvas. In the seventeenth century, the classical book on heaven came from the Puritan divine Richard Baxter (1615–1691). Entitled *The Saints' Everlasting Rest* (1649), it strove to depict in as vivid detail as possible a God-centred heaven – a heaven full of saints praising the Lord for ever and ever. While this theocentric perspective continued throughout the eighteenth century, it gradually gave way to a different, more human-centred view.[244] A first move in this direction was the assumption, so ably argued by the Jesuit Athanasius Kircher (1602–1680), that the eternal abode of the blessed must be a truly human *environment*, one in which the physical senses function, colours can be seen, sounds can be heard, and so on.[245] Increasingly, authors also insisted on the truly human character of the other *life*, imagined and described touching scenes of reunion, and spoke of heaven as home.

The general willingness to speculate about the details of eternal life can be illustrated from a quite unexpected source – James Boswell's *Life of Samuel Johnson* (1791). Dr. Johnson (1709–1784), the famous English lexicographer, was immortalised in James Boswell's charming biography that ranks among the

---

243 Anonymous author, 'Prüfungsversuch, ob es wol ausgemacht sei, daß Swedenborg zu den Schwärmern gehöre', in: Emanuel von Swedenborg, *Revision der bisherigen Theologie*, Breslau 1786, pp. iii–liv, here p. xliv. My translation; the German reads: 'Wenn er von seinen (von ihm behaupteten) Offenbarungszuständen etwas erzählet, so findet man an ihm den Geist eines mit gutem Bewußtsein beobachtenden, sehr treu und genau erzählenden Geschichtschreibers.' The anonymous author knew *De Coelo*, of which he quotes no. 358 to assert the sober, practical character of Swedenborg's ethics and to defend the seer against the reproach of sectarian enthusiasm ('Prüfungsversuch', pp. xl–xli).

244 Bernhard Lang and Colleen McDannell, *Heaven: A History*, New Haven 1988, pp. 177, 224–227.

245 Randles, *The Unmaking of the Medieval Christian Cosmos*, p. 165.

foremost works of English literature. Keen to note everything Johnson said, he recorded a dialogue the two had one evening in 1772. This is how Boswell describes the conversation:

> I [i.e., Boswell] again visited him [Dr. Johnson] at night. Finding him in a very good humour, I ventured to lead him to the subject of our situation in a future state, having much curiosity to know his notions on that point. Johnson: 'Why, Sir, the happiness of an unembodied spirit will consist in the consciousness of the favour of God, in the contemplation of truth, and in the possession of felicitating ideas.' Boswell: 'But, Sir, is there any harm in our forming to ourselves conjectures as to the particulars of our happiness, though the scripture has said but very little on the subject? We know not what we shall be.' Johnson: 'Sir, there is no harm.'[246]

The conversation then goes into these various 'particulars' of eternal happiness – meeting friends, listening to music, and having a body, for 'there are some philosophers and divines who have maintained that we shall not be spiritualized to such a degree, but that something of matter, very much refined, will remain'.[247] Both Dr. Johnson and Boswell were normal Britons of their time, interested in everything, but not overly concerned about religion. In listening to them, we can get a glimpse of the baroque spirit: it was considered normal – 'not doing any harm' – to offer speculations about heavenly life. The dialogue between the two supports the view recently suggested by Philip Almond in his study *Heaven and Hell in Enlightenment England*: in the seventeenth and eighteenth centuries, the influence of Platonic philosophers such as Henry More was pervasive and provided the background to the Boswell–Dr. Johnson dialogue. Moreover, the idea that at death the soul exchanges its terrestrial vehicle for one of air, or a more refined one of aether, was common to all Platonists of the period, including More[248] in England and Leibniz[249] in Germany.[250]

---

246 James Boswell, *Life of Johnson* [1791], Oxford 1980, p. 471.
247 Boswell, *Life of Samuel Johnson*, p. 193.
248 Philip C. Almond, *Heaven and Hell in Enlightenment England*, Cambridge 1994, pp. 29–33.
249 Swedenborg, *A Philosopher's Note Book*, p. 281.
250 That angels, spirits, and human souls all have some kind of body was believed by many philosophers and theologians in early-modern Europe. In his *Colloquium Heptaplomeres de abditis sublimium arcanis* (1596), the French political writer and jurist Jean Bodin (1530–1596) summarises the argument as follows: 'If an angel has no body, as Aristotle and most theologians think, its substance would be everywhere, and it would have a being of infinite extension. Moreover, it would follow that Intelligences and Evil Spirits could do the same as God, and so everything would be confused. [...] We have, then, a clear demonstration [...] that angels, evil spirits, and souls have bodies and limits, and that their natures are subject to change' (*The Occult in Early Modern Europe: A Documentary History*. Edited and translated by P. G. Maxwell-Stuart, New York 1999, pp. 177–178).

According to the modern Platonic school, the otherworld was not only coextensive with the physical universe; located within the universe, it shared the same spatio-temporal realm. The theory of the vehicle of the soul kept spirits, demons, and angels within the physical realm and thus capable of scientific investigation or, at least, reasonable speculation. Almond[251] describes the Platonist's map as depicting the following two levels:

1. The uppermost level is the aetherial heavenly kingdom where dwell God, the angels, the saints, and the souls of the blessed.
2. Below the heavenly kingdom is an aerial kingdom, peopled by some of the souls. Unable to penetrate into the higher levels of the aerial kingdom, the wicked soul and the evil spirits have to stay close to earth. Some of the evil spirits live in the cavities within the earth.

If the Platonists' views on eternal living are compared with those of other seventeenth- and eighteenth-century authors [as summarised above, in chapter 3, 'The Modernisation of Life after Death'], several observations can be made. *First*, that Swedenborg's *De Coelo* finds, as it were, a natural place among the baroque authors. He shares their interest in life after death and their effort to give precise descriptions of the other life. Details of his description find parallels – the motif of meeting again with friends and relatives, intimations of sexual pleasures, and the placing of dead children in heaven rather than in hell. *Second*, *De Coelo* – and its parent-work, the *Arcana Coelestia* – offers by far the most detailed description of the topic. No one prefigured Swedenborg's idea of the spiritual kingdom being an upper-class world of aristocrats, complete with fine clothing, castles, and formal parks. No one previously had the idea that there could be an even higher heaven, the heavenly kingdom, in which the angels live in primitive, noble-savage circumstances, are naked, and have simple, wooden churches.[252] *Third*, Swedenborg departs from the Platonic paradigm established by Henry More and others in that he modifies the notions of time and space in heaven and hell (nos. 162–169, 191–199). Unlike the new Platonic paradigm,

---

251 Almond, *Heaven and Hell in Enlightenment England*, pp. 36–37.
252 Swedenborg, *De Coelo*, nos. 179 and 223. In his vision of the angels living in the heavenly kingdom, Swedenborg echoes ideas of the 'noble savage' in a state of innocent piety and morality uncorrupted by urban civilization. Perhaps this underlies his statement that 'of non-Christians, the Africans are especially valued' (no. 326). For Swedenborg's view of Africa, see J. Durban Odhner, 'Reflections on Africa', *The New Philosophy* 81 (1978), pp. 255–270. Swedenborg's description of the heavenly kingdom also parallels classical descriptions of the 'Golden Age' (no. 115), on which see Scott I. Frazier, 'Echoes from the Past: A Look at Classical Influences within Swedenborg's Golden Age', *Scripta: Bryn Athyn College Review* 1 (1998), pp. 27–44.

Swedenborg does not include heaven and hell within the material universe as we know it, but rather asserts the existence of a spiritual universe connected to the physical by 'correspondences'. *Fourth*, Swedenborg is the only author who claimed to have been in contact with the other world, and was thus unique in his day. Some considered him insane, and Immanuel Kant's *Träume eines Geistersehers* (Dreams of a Spirit-Seer, 1766) with its apparently scathing critique of the Swedish visionary's work demonstrates how foreign the visionary mode was to the Enlightenment temper. For the baroque age, speculation about the other world was possible, as even Kant conceded; yet it had to be done within the limits of reason, Kant argued, for there cannot be any real experience of the beyond. As a visionary, Swedenborg announces another intellectual movement: that of Romanticism.

The dawn of the Romantic Age

In 1772, a twenty-three-year-old youth reviewed several volumes of Aussichten in die Ewigkeit (Prospects of Eternity) by Johann Kaspar Lavater (1741–1801) in a learned journal printed in Frankfurt, Germany. Although the reviewer found some interesting passages in the letters that made up this treatise on the afterlife, his overall reaction was reserved: 'In letter 17, the one on the social joys of heaven, there is a lot of warmth as well as goodness of the heart, but not enough to fill our soul with heaven.'[253] He felt that the Swiss author had dealt with an interesting subject in a cold, bloodless, pedantic manner, full of reason but lacking the fire of feeling and the contagious power of enthusiasm. The review ends on a lyrical note. The author should seek the inspiration of

> that divinely chosen seer of our age, who was impregnated by the joys of heaven, to whom the spirits spoke through all senses and the entire body, in whose bosom the angels lived: the glory of this man should radiate on him, and, if possible, set him aglow, so that he can feel the bliss and appreciate the stammering voice of the prophets whose spirit is filled with unutterable words.[254]

The young reviewer was Goethe (1749–1832), and the man he recommended, though did not name, none other than Swedenborg.[255]

---

253 Johann Wolfgang Goethe, 'Review of *Aussichten in die Ewigkeit*' [1772], in: idem, *Sämtliche Werke. Münchener Ausgabe.* Edited by K. Richter, Munich 1987, vol. 1/2, p. 384.
254 Goethe, 'Review of *Aussichten in die Ewigkeit*' [1772], p. 385.
255 Waldo C. Peebles, 'Swedenborg's Influence upon Goethe', *The Germanic Review* 8 (1933), pp. 147–156, here p. 148. That in the years 1772 and 1773 Goethe was quite willing to acknowledge the authority of a divinely inspired genius is evident not only from the Lavater

In Europe, from the middle of the eighteenth century, three intellectual and cultural movements vied with each other: the older baroque temper, represented by the pious and learned Lavater; the Enlightenment which, in the person of Kant, was critical of traditional religion, hostile to mystical claims, and insisted on the rational limits of philosophical and theological speculation; and Romanticism which, standing firmly within the Christian tradition, expressed an interest in mysticism, dreams and visionary experience, and often gave expression to its sentiments in poetry and novels. The spirit of the young Goethe was tinged with romantic sentiment, and Swedenborg combined the baroque and the romantic tempers within one single soul.[256]

Unlike their baroque predecessors, romantic minds were not satisfied with pious speculations about the hereafter. They wished to look beyond the everyday world in which people live their everyday lives, and actually experience higher worlds. According to the romantic tradition, only a thin veil divides our world from the divine realm, and dreams, mystical experiences, visions, clairvoyance, even telepathy and somnambulism were thought to give access to it. Both the uneducated and the educated believed in the existence of spirits, their activity in and influence on the material realm, and in the ability of gifted individuals to communicate with them.[257] Some dabbled in the occult arts, forming circles that eagerly sought information about the state of deceased persons through

---

review quoted above, but also from his essay 'Zwo wichtige, bisher unerörterte biblische Fragen' (Two Important, Previously Neglected Biblical Problems, 1773). This text ends with a rhetorical exhortation, addressed to those to whom God had granted experience of the divine reality: 'When the eternal Spirit casts a benign glance of his wisdom, throws a glowing spark of his love onto his chosen one, then he must make himself known and stammer what he feels. He shall make himself known, and we will honour him! Blessed are you, wherever you come from! You, who enlighten the heathens! You, who excite the nations!' (Goethe, *Sämtliche Werke. Münchener Ausgabe*, vol. 1/2, p. 443). The chosen one is Swedenborg, and the reference to 'wisdom and love' has a strong Swedenborgian ring (see, e.g., no. 158 – love and wisdom are from the Lord). Goethe presumably knew Oetinger's book on Swedenborg; in the papers of Goethe's friend Katharina von Klettenberg (1723–1774) a few pages of excerpts from Oetinger's book were found (L. Weis, 'Goethe und Swedenborg', *Goethe-Jahrbuch* 3, 1882, pp. 349–351; G.F. Fuchs, 'Zu dem Aufsatz: Von dem Himmel und der himmlischen Freude', *Goethe-Jahrbuch* 21 (1900), pp. 281–282); these excerpts represent Oetinger's German translation of *Arcana Coelestia* nos. 449–553, a text largely repeated in *De Coelo* nos. 395–414. Thus a case can be made for Goethe's indirect knowledge of at least one section of *De Coelo*.

256 See Martin Lamm, *Upplysningstidens romantik*, Stockholm 1918, who writes about a romantic current within the eighteenth-century Enlightenment, mentioning Swedenborg as one of its major representatives.
257 Diethard Sawicki, 'Die Gespenster und ihr Ancien régime: Geisterglauben als Nachtseite der Spätaufklärung', in: Monika Neugebauer-Wölk (ed.), *Aufklärung und Esoterik*, Hamburg 1999, pp. 364–396.

spiritualist mediums.[258] In Germany, two female visionaries came to unexpected fame through romantic interest in their visions: the Catholic nun Anna Katharina Emmerich (1774–1824) and the Protestant lay woman Friedericke Hauffe (1801–1829). While Sister Anna's visions were transcribed and published by the poet Clemens Brentano (1778–1842) to become classics of Catholic devotional literature, Miss Hauffe was immortalised as 'the seeress of Prevorst' by her doctor, the Swabian writer Justinus Kerner (1786–1862).

An analysis that includes Swedenborg in the Romantic Movement should at the same time emphasise that he actually belongs among that movement's forerunners and sources of inspiration. Throughout the Romantic Movement, and especially in Germany, Swedenborg's influence can be felt. The ease with which romantic writers in England, Germany, and France could appreciate Swedenborgian ideas demonstrates the inherent Romanticism of the author of *De Coelo*.

De Coelo frequently invokes visionary experience, often to illustrate abstract notions more vividly, so that the romantic spirit supplements and sometimes prevails over baroque rationality. Swedenborg's teaching on heavenly 'appearances' gives his otherworld a particularly visionary, romantic quality. The outward appearance of every angel expresses his or her inner being; thus inner goodness appears as shining beauty (no. 459), and an evil character manifests itself as visible ugliness. That the inner state creates the outer appearance is also true of the clothes the angels wear in the spiritual kingdom: the more elegant, shining, or festive the clothing, the more intelligent is that person. 'The most intelligent wear clothes that gleam as though aflame, some radiant as though alight. The less intelligent wear pure white and soft clothes that do not shine' (no. 178). The same inner-directedness is true of the environment in which the angels live, for 'in the heavens, everything comes into being from the Lord in response to the deeper nature of the angels' (no. 173). To angels focused on intelligence 'there appear gardens and parks full of all kinds of trees and flowers'; in these trees 'there are fruits in keeping with the quality of the love these intelligent angels are absorbed in' (no. 175). One may compare this psychological world to one projected by a magic lantern: the lantern and its repertoire of images correspond to the angelic soul and its states, the radiating light corresponds to divine inflow, and the projected images to the angel's environment. All inner states not only manifest themselves in the outside world, but actually create that world. In Swedenborg's words: 'It can never be said that heaven is outside anyone. It is within; because every angel accepts the heaven that is outside in keeping with the heaven that is within' (no. 54).

---

258 Sigstedt, *The Swedenborg Epic*, p. 343.

Partly due to divine inflowing, partly due to the angels' own mood, the nature of the angels is constantly changing, so that they are never exactly the same (no. 155). And the same is again true of their surroundings. The houses in which the angels live 'change slightly in response to the changes in the state of their deeper natures' (no. 190). 'As the states of the inner levels of angels' love and wisdom change, so too do the states of the various things that surround them and are visible to their eyes; for the things that surround angels are given their appearance according to the things that are within them' (no. 156). In other words: heavenly reality, though originating with the Lord, is constantly shaped and reshaped by the angels. As a result, the individual angels always find themselves in an environment congenial to their mental state, as if that environment were a projection or emanation of their inner state. In heaven, one might say, all people have heaven within themselves, and this is why Swedenborg can call each individual a complete heaven: 'Heaven is not outside angels but within them. Their deeper levels, the levels of their minds, are arranged in the form of heaven and therefore are arranged to accept all the elements of heaven that are outside them. [...] As a result, each angel is also a heaven' (no. 53).

The visionary's romantic notion of an ideal world in which everything emerges from the inner being of eternally young, beautiful men and women (no. 414) has inspired one of his most reserved biographers to acknowledge the master's achievement. 'This idea may well be the most ingenious feature of Swedenborg's eschatology', writes Martin Lamm, 'and it is in its development that his artistic achievement culminates. Thanks to his unique ability of giving symbolic meaning to a spiritual world fashioned out of earthly notions, he could give it the same fantastic, dreamlike quality which it must have had in his own original visions.'[259]

In addition to the visionary mode of experience and description, one more feature foreshadows – and eventually deeply impresses – the romantic age: the theme of heavenly love between men and women. The classical canon of Christian thought does not allow for the subject to be dealt with, for in heaven, according to standard Christian doctrine, all bliss derives from the soul's enjoyment of God alone. In baroque theology, the French Jesuit Pierre Nicole (1625–1695) summed up this teaching by saying that in heaven, the blessed will have no desire for anything else except God. Their souls' 'capacity to love, desire and enjoy will be so exhausted that it will be impossible for them to love and desire anything besides God'.[260] For Nicole, the communion of the blessed

---

259 Lamm, *Swedenborg*, p. 367. My translation from the German.
260 Pierre Nicole, *Essais de Morale*, Geneva 1971, vol. 1, p. 375. My translation.

with each other is so unimportant that he speaks of heavenly existence as *solitude eternelle avec Dieu seul:* 'The human being is created to live in an eternal solitude with God alone.'[261] During the age of the baroque, as has been shown, the classical teaching as expressed by Nicole was gradually modified, and the idea of love, even erotic love, between the blessed could be imagined. But while the subject itself occasionally surfaces in earlier writing, it never became developed to the extent it was in Swedenborg's work.

At first sight, what *De Coelo* says about men and women sounds quite conventional: 'As to the innate nature, men act on the basis of reason (*ex ratione*), while women act on the basis of their feelings (*ex affectione*). As to form, the man has a rougher and less attractive face, a deeper voice, and a stronger body, while the woman has a softer and more attractive face, a gentler voice, and a softer body' (no. 368). A closer reading reveals that Swedenborg is more nuanced than this quotation seems to suggest. Feelings, for him, are related to volition which, as has been shown, is valued more highly than the faculty of thinking and reasoning; thus *De Coelo* comes close to admitting the superiority of women. But it is not the celebration of female superiority that interests Swedenborg. He celebrates heavenly marital union as a merging of the two sexes, and the union is so complete that the two appear as one angel rather than two different beings (no. 367). Their sharing of reasoning (*ratio*) and feeling (*affectio*) is complete. 'I have been told by angels', exclaims the seer, 'that the more two spouses are engaged in this kind of union, the more they are caught up in marital love and, at the same time, in intelligence, wisdom, and happiness' (no. 370). This is the stuff of which the romantic vision of love is made. Without Swedenborg, Novalis (1772–1801) would never have described heavenly bliss in terms of 'sweet talk of whispered wishes: this is all we hear, and we gaze into blessed eyes forever, and taste nothing but mouth and kiss'.[262] Swedenborg gave Romanticism one of its most daring fantasies.

Summary

Emanuel Swedenborg's book *De Coelo et ejus mirabilibus et de Inferno, ex Auditis et Visis* (Heaven and Hell, Heard and Seen) ranks as an eighteenth-century classic on its subject. Although sometimes described simply as a sentimental book, it encompasses much more. Echoing as it does a variety of

---

261 Nicole, *Essais de Morale*, vol. 1, p. 506. My translation.
262 Novalis, 'Lied der Toten', in: *Tagebücher und Briefe*. Edited by R. Samuel, Munich 1978, vol. 1, p. 401. This 'Song of the Dead' was written in 1800 but published only posthumously.

cultural and intellectual currents, it strikes at least today's reader as a rather complex work. In building on archaic views of the permanent conflict between good and evil; adopting Neoplatonic notions of the Deity; drawing on the Renaissance appreciation of the human will and of the unashamed enjoyment of riches; describing heaven and hell in depth of detail that surpasses even that of baroque spiritual writers; and, finally, in developing bold ideas about marital love in heaven and trying to be true to the visionary experiences of his own romantic spirit, Swedenborg indeed created a work of imposing complexity.

Appendix

1688	January 22	Emanuel Swedberg born in Stockholm, Sweden
1719	May 26	The children of Bishop Jesper Swedberg were ennobled and their name changed to Swedenborg
1745	April	Swedenborg received a divine call in London
1747	July 17	Swedenborg retires from Royal Board of Mines in Sweden
1749	summer	First volume of *Arcana coelestia* (Swedenborg's main theological work) published anonymously in London
1756	June	Final volume of *Arcana coelestia* published
1758		Anonymous publication of *De Coelo* in London
1759	January 5	First reaction to *De Coelo* in short, unpublished notes by Count Gustaf Bonde, Sweden
1760	March 5	Carl Gustaf Tessin visits Swedenborg in Stockholm, talks with him about *De Coelo*
1769		Johann Christian Cuno's notes on *De Coelo*
1770	February 28	John Wesley's first diary entry on Swedenborg, with possible reference to *De Coelo*
1772	March 29	Swedenborg dies in London
		Goethe, in review of Lavater's *Aussichten in die Ewigkeit*, recommends Swedenborg's work
1775		*Vom Himmel und von den wunderbaren Dingen desselben* (German translation of *De Coelo*) published in Leipzig, Germany
1778		*A Treatise concerning Heaven and Hell* (translation of *De Coelo*) published in London
	July	*A Treatise concerning Heaven and Hell* favourably reviewed in *The Gentleman's Magazine*, London
1779	February 12	John Wesley recommends Swedenborg's work to Elizabeth Ritchie
1782		*Les Merveilles du Ciel et de l'Enfer* (French translation of *De Coelo*) published in Berlin, Germany
	January 2	Robert Hindmarsh borrows *A Treatise concerning Heaven and Hell* from a friend.
1783		John Wesley's article 'Thoughts on the Writings of Baron Swedenborg' (written May 9, 1782) published in the *Arminian Magazine*
1784		Theosophical Society founded by Robert Hindmarsh in London
		Robert Hindmarsh publishes second printing of *A Treatise concerning Heaven and Hell*

Table 5.4 Swedenborg chronology

121

Chapter 6: A Swedish Heaven in European Thought. Early Readers of Swedenborg. Appendix: Thomas Hartley on Swedenborg's Doctrine of Correspondences (1778)

> Among all visionaries, Herr Swedenborg is probably the one who has written most explicitly. He discusses, quotes sources, adduces arguments and causes, etc. The whole edifice has a kind of coherence and with all its peculiarity is erected with studied thought. The book, moreover, has so many new and unexpected turns that it may be read through without boredom.[263]
> Carl Gustaf Tessin, *Diary*, entry of July 4, 1760

Knowledge of responses to a book, especially those of the first generation of readers, is a helpful tool in understanding any literary work. In fact, modern literary criticism has made 'early reader responses' an indispensable item in its repertoire of methods. Luckily, some of the very early readers of Swedenborg's book *De Coelo et ejus mirabilibus et de Inferno, ex Auditis et Visis* (Heaven and Hell, Heard and Seen, 1758) – analysed in the previous chapter – confided their thoughts to private diaries or expressed them freely in published reviews and anecdotes. While the relevant sources are scarce, they nevertheless permit a classification of these first readers into four types: the well-born reader of the gentle class, the translator, the theologian, and the founder of a new church.

Readers of the gentle class in Sweden, Amsterdam, and London

Two Swedes and one German, all personally known to Swedenborg, fall into our first category – the educated reader of the gentle class. Writing private notes or memoirs between 1759 and 1770, Count Gustaf Bonde, Carl Gustaf Tessin, and Johann Christian Cuno have left us the earliest readers' responses to the original Latin edition of *De Coelo*. To these three gentleman readers we can add a fourth one – the anonymous reviewer of *A Treatise concerning Heaven and Hell* in the *Gentleman's Magazine* of 1778.

After having published *De Coelo*, as well as four other books, in London in 1758, Swedenborg returned to Sweden, carrying with him, it seems, only a small

---

263 Carl Gustaf Tessin, quoted in Cyriel Odhner Sigstedt, *The Swedenborg Epic: The Life and Work of Emanuel Swedenborg*, London 1981, pp. 274–275.

number of copies of his new publications.[264] One copy came into Sweden through unknown channels and was sold to Count Gustaf Bonde (1682–1764), then chancellor of the University of Uppsala, an old acquaintance of Swedenborg. Bonde or his bookseller must have been the first in Sweden to guess or find out that Swedenborg was the author of the anonymously printed work.

In a personal, unpublished note of uncertain date – 1759 or 1760 – Count Bonde lists several objections after reading *De Coelo*.[265] Swedenborg's teaching that 'our nature after death depends on the kind of life we led in the world' (heading of nos. 470–484) seemed to contradict 'our principle articles of faith and the hope of everlasting life for a poor sinner'. Lutherans believe in the essential sinfulness of every human being, so that, were Swedenborg right, all of them would end in hell. According to Bonde, Swedenborg fails to consider Christ's merit and God's merciful intervention on behalf of the sinner. It is not the life we lead on earth, Bonde contends, but God's mercy that determines life everlasting; therefore there is the hope of everlasting life even for a poor sinner. Other Swedenborgian views were equally problematic: how could the serpent have tempted Eve in paradise, if there were no angels and devils before human beings existed in paradise? The count fears that if, instead of basing one's faith on the plain letter of Scripture, one has to look into it for an 'internal sense', then anyone could make up a special religion to suit himself, by searching out whatever meaning he pleases. What especially struck Count Bonde was Swedenborg's criticism of the Lutheran doctrine of 'salvation by faith through divine mercy' (see nos. 521 and 522) and his redefinition of angels that amounted to a dismissal of traditional beliefs in angels as a separate, non-human species within God's creation (no. 311). Interestingly, Bonde does not seem to have been surprised by the author's claim of contact with angels. Bonde's Lutheran beliefs were tolerant of angelic revelations, but intolerant of everything that contradicted the doctrine of divine mercy.

Another very early reader and diarist was Carl Gustaf Tessin (1695–1770), an architect and former president of the House of Nobles in Sweden. His surviving

---

264 Rudolf Leonhard Tafel, *Documents concerning the Life and Character of Emanuel Swedenborg*, London 1890, vol. 2/3, p. 397; Alfred Acton, *The Letters and Memorials of Emanuel Swedenborg*, Bryn Athyn, Penn. 1955, vol. 2, p. 529.

265 The short document is in the State Archives of Stockholm; a transcript can be found in the Academy Collection of Swedenborg Documents, vol. 6, no. 809 (Swedenborg Library, Bryn Athyn, Pennsylvania). The Academy Collection dates the document to 1760, whereas Cyriel Odhner Sigstedt (*The Swedenborg Epic: The Life and Work of Emanuel Swedenborg*, London 1981, p. 270) proposes January 5, 1759.

diary includes several notes on Swedenborg. The first records Tessin's visit to Swedenborg in Stockholm:

> Merely out of curiosity, to make the acquaintance of a singular man, I went to see Assessor Swedenborg on the afternoon of March 5, 1760. He lives far up on Hornsgatan in a neat little wooden house on a large plot of ground with a garden belonging to him. I found there an old man about seventy-three years of age with a countenance perfectly like that of the late Bishop Swedberg, but not so tall. He had feeble eyes, a large mouth, and a pale complexion, but he was cheerful, friendly, and talkative. It seemed that I was welcome, and as I had not intended to make many preludes, I began at once by speaking about the work on *Heaven and Hell*.[266]

Tessin apparently had heard about this book, but he had not seen a copy. Swedenborg had to tell him that at that time, no copies were available in Sweden:

> He [Swedenborg] said that besides his own copy he had only two others, which he had intended, at the next Riksdag [meeting of parliament], to hand over to two bishops; but as he had heard that one copy of it had come into the country without his knowledge, having been sold to His Excellency Count Bonde, he had reconsidered the matter and given one of his copies to Senator Count Höpken and the other one to Councillor Oelreich, the censor of books. He expects fifty more copies from England next spring and then he will send one to me.[267]

These fifty copies must have arrived promptly, and by July, he had his own copy of *De Coelo*. In a diary entry of July 4, 1760 Tessin comments on the book:

> Among all visionaries, Herr Swedenborg is probably the one who has written most explicitly. He discusses, quotes sources, adduces arguments and causes, etc. The whole edifice has a kind of coherence and with all its peculiarity is erected with studied thought. The book, moreover, has so many new and unexpected turns that it may be read through without boredom. What he says in no. 191 [...] concerning space in heaven is a well-reasoned dream. Throughout the entire work one recognizes Bishop Swedberg's son, who is dreaming with far greater profundity than the father [...] All this may be read with the same credence one gives to Mohammed's Alkoran.[268]

---

266 Tessin, as quoted in Sigstedt, *The Swedenborg Epic*, p. 273. See also Tafel, *Documents*, vol. 2/3, pp. 398–399.

267 Tessin, as quoted in Sigstedt, *The Swedenborg Epic*, p. 273. See also Tafel, *Documents*, vol. 2/3, p. 399.

268 Tessin, as quoted in Sigstedt, *The Swedenborg Epic*, pp. 274–275. – The transcript in the Academy Collection of Swedenborg Documents, vol. 6, no. 793.12 (Swedenborg Library, Bryn Athyn, Pennsylvania) indicates that all three passages cited here were written on March 5, 1760. Sigstedt, however, cites the date of this particular entry as July 4, 1760; and it should be noted that she copied all these entries from the original diaries of Count Tessin in his family library at Åkerö Castle in Södermanland in 1915. See Sigstedt, *The Swedenborg Epic*, pp. 465–466, notes 443 and 447.

Carl Gustaf Tessin read *De Coelo* with much interest, recognised its coherence, appreciated its novelty and even profundity, but eventually decided to place it with the Qur'an – a book of other people's revelation, a book not accepted and acceptable as *our* normative source of religion. The reference to the Qur'an was to become standard in anti-Swedenborg polemics; it will also appear in the discussion below of the reactions of Johann Christian Cuno and John Wesley, but Tessin's note of 1760 seems to be the first attestation.[269]

Johann Christian Cuno (1708–1796) – the third and final reader to be mentioned in this section – was a well-educated German merchant and author living in Amsterdam. In the mid-nineteenth century, the librarian of the Royal Library in Brussels was alerted to the existence of a German autographic manuscript of four thousand folio pages – the autobiography of Cuno. August Scheler, the librarian, read the manuscript and decided to publish the section dealing with Swedenborg.[270]

Cuno happened to meet Swedenborg in an Amsterdam bookstore on November 4, 1768, and the two men took a liking to each other. At the time, Swedenborg was living in Amsterdam to supervise the printing of some of his books, and it was in this city that Cuno became one of his friends and avid readers. Between 1768 and 1770, he saw Swedenborg frequently, and he often had the opportunity to ask questions about his religious views and his publications. Cuno owned some of Swedenborg's books; others – including *De Coelo* – he borrowed from the author.[271] He read *De Coelo* in 1769, 'eleven years' after its publication,[272] took many notes, jotted down comments, and included all of them in his autobiography. A pious man, regular church-goer, and an author himself of religious books, Cuno was fully conversant with theology and immediately realised that *De Coelo* departed from the general understanding of biblical teaching.[273] He noted that in Swedenborg's theology all the angels and evil spirits were formerly human beings; there are marriages in heaven; resurrection actually means the introduction into the world of spirits. He also suspected that the author fell into the trap of Manichaeism, a heresy that posits the eternal coexistence of two conflicting principles, one good and one evil – the

---

269 The implication of the comparison to the Qur'an is that of a heavenly paradise that is too sensuous. Eighteenth-century writers often refer to the Qur'an or 'Mahometans' when rejecting sensuous notions of heaven; for an example, see *The Gentleman's Magazine* 9 (1739), p. 5b, quoted above, p. 41.
270 Johann Christian Cuno, *Memoirs on Swedenborg*. Translated from German by C.E. Berninger, Bryn Athyn, Penn. 1947.
271 Cuno, *Memoirs on Swedenborg*, p. 17.
272 Cuno, *Memoirs on Swedenborg*, p. 52.
273 Cuno, *Memoirs on Swedenborg*, pp. 43–68.

one realised in heaven, the other in hell. Cuno considered Swedenborg's visionary claims the most questionable feature of his friend's theology. Is it likely that a gentleman of the eighteenth century could be superior to St Paul, who had been unable to tell of his heavenly visions? Swedenborg himself had written about enthusiasts who, with their minds focused exclusively on matters of religion, delved into the world of spirits and were deceived by lying spirits (no. 249). Is it possible that Swedenborg, despite his claims to the contrary, belongs with these enthusiasts?[274]

Nevertheless, Cuno admits to finding 'here and there [...] a grain of gold'.[275] He appreciated what Swedenborg wrote about the admission of the wise and virtuous pagans like Cicero into heaven.[276] All things considered, however, doubts remain:

> I myself [Cuno] cannot in the least defend the upright Swedenborg. But if, eleven years ago, when this work of his whereof I am speaking, namely *Heaven and Hell* was published, a well-grounded theologian had left what is good therein in its place, and soberly refuted what was erroneous and contradictory, then the good man, if not diverted from his imaginations, would nevertheless have been constrained to be more careful in the future, and not to flood the world with his multifarious writings.[277]

If the statements of Bonde, Tessin, and Cuno were representative of the opinions of early readers of *De Coelo*, then one would have to say that the response was largely critical and only marginally appreciative. There were other readers, however, and some of them responded in a friendly way, if not with enthusiasm. When the first English translation of *De Coelo* became available in 1778, a then-fashionable monthly publication, *The Gentleman's Magazine* of London, honoured it with a review of a little more than two columns in small print. The anonymous reviewer offered extensive excerpts from the translator's preface to introduce Swedenborg (spelled 'Swedenberg' in the review), the scientist and visionary.[278] A tantalisingly brief comment on *A Treatise concerning Heaven and Hell* summarily concluded:

> We shall only observe, upon the whole, that whatever judgment the public may entertain of the visionary part of this work, the doctrinal part is unexceptionable; and as the former has met with a very able advocate in the preface-writer, the latter will need no justification.[279]

---

274 Cuno, *Memoirs on Swedenborg*, p. 114.
275 Cuno, *Memoirs on Swedenborg*, 97.
276 Cuno, *Memoirs on Swedenborg*, p. 52.
277 Cuno, *Memoirs on Swedenborg*, p. 52.
278 To some readers of *The Gentleman's Magazine*, Swedenborg was not unknown. The April 1772 number – vol. 42, p. 198b – includes the following obituary note: 'Hon. and learned Emanuel Swedenburgh [sic], famous for his mathematical works, and for his visionary [works].'
279 *The Gentleman's Magazine* vol. 48 (1778), p. 326b.

No contemporary reader would have missed the friendly tone of the review, and so we may conclude that in 1778, when the first public statement on Swedenborg's book appeared, the educated readers of England took the work seriously. Regrettably, no information about the reviewer can be found in the surviving files of the publisher.[280] By contrast, the name of the 'very able advocate' who wrote the preface of *A Treatise concerning Heaven and Hell* has been determined: Thomas Hartley. He belongs among those of the early readers of *De Coelo* whose enthusiasm led them to produce vernacular versions of the Latin book.

Early translators

Swedenborg's book had the chance to capture the interest not only of people of the gentle class with a passing interest in the subject, but also of pious men who sought to promote it in vernacular translations. Soon, *De Coelo* became *Vom Himmel und von den wunderbaren Dingen desselben* (1775, German), *A Treatise concerning Heaven and Hell* (1778), and *Les Merveilles du Ciel et de l'Enfer* (1782, French).

The first to translate *De Coelo* was a German. Although *Vom Himmel und von den wunderbaren Dingen desselben* does not mention the translator's name, a contemporary German biographical dictionary attributes it to Johann Christoph Lenz (1748–1791) who is identified as the clerk and master accountant of the University of Leipzig.[281] Lenz must have owned a sizeable collection of books he classified as 'alchemistic and theosophical works'.[282] Most likely, he found Swedenborg's books more interesting than others and therefore chose two of them for translation: *De Commercia Animae et Corporis*, which appeared as *Von der Vereinigung der Seele und des Leibes* (1772) and *De Coelo*, issued as *Vom Himmel* (1775).

Hartley and Cookworthy, the two English translators, knew Swedenborg personally and admired him, and their work made an enormous impact on many readers. Thomas Hartley (1709–1784) was an Anglican cleric. As an absentee rector of Winwick, Northhamptonshire, he paid a curate to do the regular parish

---

280 James M. Kuist, *The Nichols File of* The Gentleman's Magazine: *Attributions of Authorship and Other Documentation in Editorial Papers at the Folger Library*, Madison, Wisc. 1982.
281 Georg Christoph Hamburger and Johann Georg Meusel (eds.), *Das gelehrte Teutschland; oder Lexikon der jetzt lebenden Schriftsteller*. 5th ed., Lemgo 1797, vol. 4, entry on 'Lenz, Johann Christoph'.
282 Reinhard Breymeyer, 'Ein radikaler Pietist im Umkreis des jungen Goethe', in: *Pietismus und Neuzeit* 9 (1984), pp. 180–237, here p. 227.

work. Liberated from that duty, Hartley led the life of an intellectual and a writer interested in mysticism. He was acquainted with Selina, Countess of Huntingdon (1707–1791), the famous patroness of English baroque spirituality, as well as William Law (1686–1761) and George Whitfield 1714–1770).[283] William Cookworthy (1705–1780), otherwise a busy chemist, porcelain manufacturer, and entrepreneur, found time to serve the Quaker community of Plymouth as an elder.[284] During the 1760s, the two came to be interested in Swedenborg's work, eventually meeting each other and becoming friends, and they also visited the master in London. Their story is one of devotion to the work of Swedenborg. After Swedenborg's death, the two men collaborated on the translation of *De Coelo*. Although Rev. Hartley was then a frail old man of over seventy, he reworked Cookworthy's draft. In 1778 Cookworthy had it published at his own expense, paying one hundred pounds sterling to the printer.[285]

Hartley wrote a long introduction to *A Treatise concerning Heaven and Hell* in which he defended Swedenborg's claim to have knowledge of the spiritual world from experience.[286] He knew that his times were not favourable to such claims, for 'the belief of all extraordinary or supernatural dispensations is at a very low ebb with us'.[287] Contemporaries of Hartley would – and in one case known to him, actually did – obtain for persons who conversed with angels a 'statute of lunacy' and order them to the madhouse.[288] This attitude not only rested on 'an undue exaltation of man's natural rational faculties and powers, as the sufficient test of revealed Truth', but also on the belief that miracles ceased some time during the early church.[289] This, however, cannot be true, for it does not seem to be rational to dismiss all the many reports of miracles and visions known from all periods of church history as inventions and forgeries.[290] Thus Hartley felt that he could appeal to popular belief as if to common knowledge when defending the reality of otherworldly contacts:

---

283 A.E. Beilby, *Rev. Thomas Hartley, A.M.*, London 1931.
284 A. Douglas Selleck, *Cookworthy and His Circle*, Plymouth 1978.
285 Tafel, *Documents*, vol. 2/2, p. 539.
286 The introduction to *A Treatise concerning Heaven and Hell* is anonymous, but scholars generally admit Hartley's authorship. *The Gentleman's Magazine* 61 (1791), pp. 619b–620a prints a letter by 'Candidus'. Candidus recommends to a correspondent, who inquired after the true character of Swedenborg, to read the preface of *A Treatise concerning Heaven and Hell*, stating that it was 'written by the Rev. T. Hartley, a worthy and pious clergyman of the Church of England' (620a).
287 Thomas Hartley, Preface to Swedenborg, *A Treatise concerning Heaven and Hell*, London 1778, pp. i–liii, here p. vi.
288 Hartley, Preface, p. xviii.
289 Hartley, Preface, p. vi.
290 Hartley, Preface, p. xiii.

> And who will say, that the natural eye of man is incapable [...] to discern the subtle vehicles of certain spirits, whether consisting of air or ether; certain it is, that either by condensation, or some other way, they can make themselves visible, and converse with us, as man with man, and so innumerable are the instances hereof, as also of their discoveries, warnings, predictions, &c. that I may venture to affirm, with an appeal to the publick for the truth of it, that there are few ancient families in any county of Great Britain, that are not possessed of records or traditions of the same in their own houses, however the prevailing Sadducism of these times may have sunk the credit of them, as well as in great measure cut off communications of this kind.[291]

For many contemporaries of Hartley, this was a fragile argument. In Britain, the 'Cock Lane' case of 1762 had left its mark on people's memory.[292] In January 1762, Fanny Lynes, who had recently died of smallpox, allegedly made herself known in the house of Richard Parsons in Cock Lane, London. Through peculiar knockings heard in one room, she was allegedly indicating that she had been murdered. All of London discussed the case, and the investigating committee included celebrities like Dr. Samuel Johnson. Soon however, the 'Cock Lane ghost' could be exposed as a hoax. By 1778, the case had not been forgotten, but in Britain belief in ghosts was too firmly established in popular lore to be eradicated by the exposure of one case of fraud. The anonymous reviewer of *A Treatise concerning Heaven and Hell* quotes Hartley's appeal to British ghost-seeing without indicating any reservations against it.[293]

Hartley ends his long preface with an explanation of two of Swedenborg's teachings: the doctrine of 'correspondences' and the doctrine of the intermediate state in which the departed find themselves between death and relegation to either heaven or hell. Since Hartley's explanation of 'correspondences' can indeed help elucidate *De Coelo*, we felt we should append an excerpt to the present introduction (see below, *Appendix*). By way of conclusion, here are Hartley's recommendations about reading *A Treatise concerning Heaven and Hell*. One can understand Swedenborg as 'the enlightened Seer, and the extraordinary messenger of important news from the other world'; failing this, one may consider him as a 'Christian divine and sage interpreter of the Scriptures'. Failing this again, one may 'read him as a the judicious moralist, and acute metaphysician; or read him as the profound philosopher; or if he cannot please in any of these characters, read him at least as the ingenious author of a divine romance'.[294]

---

291 Hartley, Preface, pp. xxii–xxiii.
292 Jenny Uglow, *Hogarth: A Life and a World*, London 1997, pp. 625–655.
293 *The Gentleman's Magazine* 1778, p. 326a.
294 Hartley, Preface, p. xxxviii.

The translation of *De Coelo* by Cookworthy and Hartley made a great impact on at least some contemporaries – both positively and negatively. We know of two important readers of this translation. Both Robert Hindmarsh and John Wesley read *A Treatise concerning Heaven and Hell* early in 1782, and, as will become clear, came to vastly different conclusions. But before commenting on these two early readers, we will comment on another early translator, Abbé Pernety.

The life of Antoine Joseph Pernety (1716–1801), the French translator of *De Coelo*, was marked by the unrest of a man who moved from a Benedictine monastery to the court of a prince; at the same time, the devout Catholic became a writer on esoteric themes.[295] In the same year in which Swedenborg had *De Coelo* printed, Pernety published his *Fables égyptiennes et grecques dévoilées et réduites au même principe* (Fables of the Egyptians and Greeks Revealed and Reduced to a Common Principle, Paris 1758). Pernety came to Prussia during the reign of Frederick the Great and served in the position of librarian between 1767 and 1783. It was as a librarian that he came across Swedenborg's work; in 1779 he read *Delitiae sapientiae de Amore conjugiali*. In his correspondence with Carl Fredrick Nordenskjöld, a Swede, he reports how he became convinced of the value and spiritual truth of Swedenborg's work. Pernety had gathered around himself a group of people interested in the esoteric arts, with whom he practiced a kind of oracle. His Neoplatonic worldview did not permit him to communicate directly with the One, the Supreme Deity; but one of the emanations of the One, called '*la Sainte Parole*' (the Holy Word), could be contacted by an oracular procedure. The answer to his question about Swedenborg was entirely favourable: Swedenborg had spoken truthfully ('*il a dit vrai*'), Sainte Parole opined.[296] As a result, Pernety produced a somewhat free French version of *De Coelo*, and the two volumes of *Les Merveilles du Ciel et de l'Enfer* were printed in Berlin in 1782.

Pernety's translation includes a long preface entitled 'Observations ou Notes sur Swédenborg' in which Pernety comments on Swedenborg's life and work. Some of the anecdotes about the author of *De Coelo* must have come to Pernety from his Swedish correspondents, the Nordenskjöld brothers, Carl Fredrick and

---

295 Williams-Hogan, 'Emanuel Swedenborg and Western Esotericism', in: Antoine Faivre et al. (eds.), *Western Esotericism and the Science of Religion*, Leuven 1998, pp. 201–252, here pp. 235–239.
296 Pernety is quoted in Williams-Hogan, 'Emanuel Swedenborg and Western Esotericism', p. 236. For a transcript of the original letter of October 20, 1781, in which the quotation appears, see Antoine Joseph Pernety, in: *Academy Collection of Swedenborg Documents*, vol. 10, no. 1663.18 (Swedenborg Library, Bryn Athyn, Penn.). For more on Pernety, see Tafel, *Documents*, vol. 1, p. 637.

August. One of the anecdotes deals with the question of whether Swedenborg's views were compatible with those of the German mystic Jacob Boehme (1575–1624). 'He was a good man, answered Swedenborg; it is a pity that some errors crept into his writings, especially with regard to the Trinity.' Similarly, Swedenborg was asked whether there was any truth in Hermetic philosophy: 'Yes, he replied, I consider it to be true, and one of the greatest wonders of God; but I advise no one to work in this subject.'[297] While we have no way of authenticating these anecdotes, we know that they reflect the interest of both August Nordenskjöld and Pernety in esoteric traditions.[298]

In obedience to *la Sainte Parole* Pernety eventually left Berlin and travelled south in order to establish the kingdom of the New Jerusalem. The nucleus of that kingdom was to be an esoteric society which he founded in the city of Avignon in Provence.

Little is known about the early reception of *Les Merveilles du Ciel et de l'Enfer*, but one anecdote deserves to be told. The French writer Honoré de Balzac knew the book, and when in 1832 he wrote his novel *Louis Lambert* – the story of a young genius – he put it in the hands of his protagonist. Aged only fourteen, Louis, a tanner's son, was found by Madame de Staël reading 'une traduction du *Ciel et de l'Enfer*'.[299] The year is 1811, and Balzac adds that at this time only a handful of French intellectuals had heard of Swedenborg. In the story, Madame de Staël takes pity on the poor boy and pays for his schooling in a near-by convent. Balzac gives us the full reading list of his genius: when Madame found him, he had already complemented his Bible studies by reading the great mystics – saint Teresa of Avila, Madame Guyon, and *Les Merveilles du Ciel et de l'Enfer*.[300] This, Balzac imagines, is how mystical life begins. And in fact, some of the philosophical thoughts with which Balzac ends his novel betray Swedenborg's influence.[301]

---

297 Antoine Joseph Pernety, 'Observations ou notes sur Swédenborg', in: Swedenborg, *Les Merveilles du Ciel et de l'Enfer*, vol. 1, Berlin 1782, pp. 64–98, here p. 78; Tafel, *Documents*, vol. 1, p. 62.
298 Swedenborg may have echoed Augustine who in the *City of God* (VIII, 23) suggests that Hermes 'makes many statements agreeable to the truth concerning the one true God, maker of the world'.
299 Honoré de Balzac, *Louis Lambert* [1832], in: idem, *La Comédie humaine*. Edited by P.-G. Castex, Paris 1980, vol. 11, p. 595.
300 Balzac, *Louis Lambert*, p. 594.
301 Lynn R. Wilkinson, *The Dream of an Absolute Language: Emanuel Swedenborg and French Literary Culture*, Albany, N.Y. 1996, pp. 156–171.

A theological reader: John Wesley

Awesome supernatural visions of God and angels, communion with spirits, sensing angelic presence and help—all of this was reported by John Wesley's entourage.[302] John Wesley (1703–1791) was fond of angels and believed that they send messages into our consciousness, sometimes during sleep, but sometimes also when we are awake.[303] The founder of the Methodist movement avidly believed in signs and wonders. It does not come as a surprise that Wesley, when he heard of Swedenborg, was intrigued by his otherworldly experience. Although both Wesley and Swedenborg lived in England, had heard of each other, and took an interest in each other's work, they never met. Shortly before his death in 1772, Swedenborg had sent him a copy of *Vera Christiana Religio* (True Christianity, 1771).[304]

Wesley's experience of reading Swedenborg's work can be followed in his private diary from February 28, 1770, where he reports that he 'sat down to read and seriously consider some of the writings of Baron Swedenborg'.[305] Although Wesley does not state which works he looked at, it may well be that *De Coelo* was among them. In his diary entry of December 8, 1771 he comes back to the subject: 'I read a little more of that strange book, Baron Swedenborg's *Theologia Coelestis.*'[306] The Latin title that he gives (which means The Theology of Heaven) seems to be a somewhat inaccurate version of the actual title, *De Coelo*, although it could also refer to *Arcana Coelestia*. Then Wesley seems to have abandoned his reading of the Baron for many years. He resumed it only after having received some English versions of Swedenborg's books. His collection now included *A Treatise concerning Heaven and Hell*, the English translation of *De Coelo*, published in 1778. His diary entry of April 22, 1779 is longer and more detailed than the earlier ones, and refers to *A Treatise concerning Heaven and Hell* as 'Baron Swedenborg's *Account of Heaven and Hell*'[307] – in his diary, Wesley cared little about noting the exact titles of books he was reading.

---

302 Stanley Ayling, *John Wesley*, London 1979, pp. 300–303.
303 John Wesley, letter to Hester Ann Roe, December 9, 1781, in: idem, *The Works*. Edited by Th. Jackson, London 1856, vol. 13, p. 77.
304 Wesley, 'Thoughts on the Writings of Baron Swedenborg' [1782], in: idem, *The Works*, vol. 13, pp. 401–422, here p. 403.
305 Wesley, *The Journal*. Edited by N. Curnock, London n.d., vol. 5, p. 345.
306 Wesley *The Journal*, vol. 5, p. 440.
307 Wesley, *The Journal*, vol. 6, p. 230.

133

1	diary	Febr. 28, 1770	positive: 'I began with huge prejudice in his favour, knowing him to be a pious man' – negative: 'entertaining madman'; possible reference to *De Coelo*	Wesley, *The Journal*, vol. 5, pp. 354–355
2	diary	Dec. 8, 1771	positive: 'It surely contains many excellent things' – negative: 'society of lunatics [...] majestic, though in ruin'; probable reference to *De Coelo*	Wesley, *The Journal*, vol. 5, p. 440
3	letter	Febr. 12, 1779	positive: 'strong and beautiful thoughts, and may be read with profit' – negative: 'majestic, though in ruins'; possible reference to *A Treatise concerning Heaven and Hell*	Wesley, *The Works*, vol. 13, p. 58
4	diary	April 22, 1779	positive: 'a man of piety, of a strong understanding' – negative: 'brain-sick man [...] essentially and dangerously wrong'; reference to *A Treatise concerning Heaven and Hell*	Wesley, *The Journal*, vol. 6, pp. 230–231
5	article	May 9, 1782	positive: [nothing] – negative: 'filthy dreamer [...] let none of you that fear God recommend such a writer any more'; reference to *A Treatise concerning Heaven and Hell*	Wesley, *The Works*, vol. 13, pp. 401–422

Table 6.1 Wesley's comments on Swedenborg

Between 1770 and early 1779, Wesley always found something positive in Swedenborg's works, even though he had his doubts and applied to him, what Milton wrote on Satan: 'His mind has not yet lost all its original brightness, but appears majestic, though in ruin.'[308] Despite this caution, his overall comments could be quite positive. In a letter addressed to his friend Miss Elizabeth Ritchie he found the following words: 'I have abundant proof that Baron Swedenborg's fever,[309] which he had thirty years before he died, much affected his

---

308 Wesley, *The Journal*, vol. 5, p. 440. See John Milton, *Paradise Lost* II, 305.
309 Wesley repeatedly refers to this 'fever' (Wesley, *The Journal*, vol. 5, p. 440; vol. 6, p. 230; Wesley, 'Thoughts on the Writings of Baron Swedenborg', p. 402). Apparently answering Wesley, Hartley, Preface, xxxii, dismisses the 'fever' incident as evidence of Swedenborg's insanity. Recent scholarship considers Wesley's source as apocryphal and doubtful, see Samuel J. Rogal, 'Swedenborg and the Wesleyans: Opposition or Outgrowth?', in: Erland J. Brock (ed.), *Swedenborg and His Influence*, Bryn Athyn, Penn. 1988, pp. 295–307, here pp. 297–298.

understanding. Yet his tract is *majestic, though in ruins*. He has strong and beautiful thoughts, and may be read with profit by a serious and cautious reader.'[310] Wesley does not specify which 'tract' he meant, but the reference may be to *A Treatise concerning Heaven and Hell*, the book recently published in English. While Wesley's letter dated February 12, 1779 cautiously recommends Swedenborg, his diary entry of April 22, 1779 comes close to a total condemnation: 'Of this work [that is, *A Treatise concerning Heaven and Hell*] in particular I must observe that the doctrine contained therein is not only quite unproved, quite precarious from beginning to end, as depending entirely on the assertion of a single brain-sick man; but that, in many instances, it is contrary to Scripture, to reason, and to itself.'[311]

It was not until early 1782 that John Wesley took the time to consider all the Swedenborg books which had accumulated in his study: *The True Christian Religion* (vol. 1; first English edition of 1781), *A Treatise concerning Heaven and Hell* (English edition of 1778), and *Delitiae sapientiae de Amore conjugiali* (which latter he refers to as *De Nuptiis Coelestibus*, with characteristic disregard for exact citation; Latin edition of 1768). His 'Thoughts on the Writings of Baron Swedenborg', completed May 9, 1782 and printed in 1783 in the *Arminian Magazine*, represent his only public statement on the subject. Here Wesley reviews Swedenborg's life, offers a selection of excerpts from Swedenborg's books, and ends with a detailed, nine-page review of *A Treatise concerning Heaven and Hell*. Compared with the diary entries, the tone has not changed. Again, Swedenborg is accused of insanity and his theology considered unacceptable. From Wesley's review, the following list of the most serious of Swedenborg's errors can be abstracted:

1. Swedenborg does not believe in the divine Trinity, but only in one God.
2. He rejects the common belief that God created angels as such. 'This grand position, which runs through all his Works, that all angels and devils were once men, without which his whole hypothesis falls to the ground, is palpably contrary to scripture.'[312]
3. He believes in a kind of purgation of certain souls after death, thereby coming close to affirming Catholic beliefs. 'How exceeding[ly] small is the difference between the Romish and the Mystic purgatory!'[313]

---

310 Wesley, letter to Elizabeth Ritchie, February 12, 1779, in: idem, *The Works*, vol. 13, p. 58.
311 Wesley, *The Journal*, vol. 6, p. 231.
312 Wesley, 'Thoughts on the Writings of Baron Swedenborg', p. 416.
313 Wesley, 'Thoughts on the Writings of Baron Swedenborg', p. 415.

4. He believes in marriages in heaven. Wesley asks, 'How is this consistent with our Lord's words, *In the resurrection they neither marry, nor are given in marriage, but are as the angels of god in heaven?*'[314]
5. He describes caverns in rocks, subterraneous mines, ruined houses, and rude cottages in hell. 'But how does this agree with what we read in the Scripture concerning hell-fire?'[315] According to Revelation 20:15, 'whosoever is not found written in the book of life, will be cast into the lake of fire'.[316]
6. He describes, especially in *The True Christian Religion*, a relatively decent life in hell: a life in which people work, rest, and even entertain themselves with the opposite sex.[317] Here Swedenborg appears as 'a filthy dreamer [...], who takes care to provide harlots, instead of fire and brimstone, for the devils and damned spirits in hell'.[318] 'So the Christian Koran exceeds even the Mahometan! Mahomet allowed such to be in paradise; but he never thought of placing them in hell.'[319] 'O how much more comfortable is the condition of these spirits in hell, than that of the galley-slaves at Marseilles, or the Indians in the mines of Potosi!'[320] Wesley considers Swedenborg's description of hell 'the most dangerous part of all his writings', for it 'tends to familiarise it to unholy men, to remove all their terror, and to make them consider it, not as a place of torment, but a very tolerable habitation'.[321]

Apart from these flagrant errors, Wesley is dissatisfied with the style of the *Treatise concerning Heaven and Hell*, for it lacks dignity. Of Swedenborg's description of heaven, Wesley writes:

> It would be tedious to point out the particular oddities and absurdities. [...] It may suffice to remark in general, that it contains nothing sublime, nothing worthy of the dignity of the subject. Most of the images are low, and mean, and earthly, not raising, but sinking, the mind of the reader; representing the very angels of God in such a light, as might move us, not to worship, but despise them. And there is a grossness and coarseness in the whole description of

---

314 Wesley, 'Thoughts on the Writings of Baron Swedenborg', p. 416, quoting Matthew 22:30.
315 Wesley, 'Thoughts on the Writings of Baron Swedenborg', p. 418.
316 Wesley, 'Thoughts on the Writings of Baron Swedenborg', p. 422.
317 In hell, each man 'is also informed that every one is at liberty to walk, to converse, and afterwards to sleep, when he hath done his Work; He is then led into an inner Part of the Cavern, where there are Harlots, and he is permitted to take one to himself, and to call her his Wife, but he is forbid on pain of Punishment, to connect himself with more than one'. Swedenborg, *True Christian Religion*. Translated by J. Clowes, London 1781, p. 344 (no. 281, 10).
318 Wesley, 'Thoughts on the Writings of Baron Swedenborg', p. 422.
319 Wesley, 'Thoughts on the Writings of Baron Swedenborg', p. 421.
320 Wesley, 'Thoughts on the Writings of Baron Swedenborg', p. 420.
321 Wesley, 'Thoughts on the Writings of Baron Swedenborg', p. 417.

the invisible world, which I am afraid will exceedingly tend to confirm rational infidels in a total disbelief of it.[322]

Elsewhere, he exclaims: 'How egregiously trifling is this account! So puerile, so far beneath the importance of the subject, that one who did not know the character of the writer [i.e., Swedenborg], might naturally imagine he was turning it into burlesque.'[323]

At an age at which John Wesley tended to look back to his own achievements, he felt unable to adopt any of Swedenborg's views. Wesley's own theology of heaven and hell was quite conventional. Long ago, he had included an abridgement of Richard Baxter's *Saints' Everlasting Rest* in his fifty-volume set entitled *A Christian Library* (1749–1755). In Baxter's heaven, the saints rest and praise God, rather than engaging in the more earthly employments described by Swedenborg. Apparently, the only result of Wesley's renewed consideration of Swedenborg's work was that he took up the subject of angels and hell in several sermons, in which he repeated fairly conventional views.[324] In Methodist circles, Swedenborg was to be *persona non grata*. 'O my brethren', Wesley addressed the Methodist readers of the *Arminian Magazine*, 'let none of you recommend such a writer any more!'[325]

Founder of a new church: Robert Hindmarsh

Wesley, a man in his old age, could not easily be impressed and shaken out of his long-standing, largely traditional theological views. When we turn to Robert Hindmarsh, we get a completely different – in many ways an opposite – story. At the impressionable age of twenty-two, Robert Hindmarsh (1759–1835), a printer, became acquainted with George Keen, a Quaker interested in Swedenborg. Keen loaned two books by Swedenborg to Robert on January 2, 1782, a day Hindmarsh remembered well: it was the very day he met his future wife, Sarah Paramor (1761?–1833). The two works were: *A Treatise concerning Heaven and Hell*, and *On the Commerce between the Soul and the Body* (both translated by Hartley). Hindmarsh immediately read the two volumes and instantly became convinced of their 'heavenly origin'.[326] He quickly became a convinced follower

---

322 Wesley, 'Thoughts on the Writings of Baron Swedenborg', p. 417.
323 Wesley, 'Thoughts on the Writings of Baron Swedenborg', p. 419.
324 Three sermons dating from 1782/83 are titled 'Of Good Angels', 'Of Evil Angels', and 'Of Hell' , see Wesley, *The Works*. Edited by A.C. Outler, Nashville 1986, vol. 3, pp. 3–44.
325 Wesley, 'Thoughts on the Writings of Baron Swedenborg', p. 422.
326 Robert Hindmarsh, *Rise and Progress of the New Jerusalem Church*. Edited by J. Madeley, London 1861, p. 23.

of Swedenborg. By 1784, he had founded an association 'instituted for the purpose of promoting the heavenly doctrines of the New Jerusalem, by translating, printing, and publishing the theological writings of the honourable Emanuel Swedenborg'.[327] With its seat in London, this 'Theosophical Society' soon boasted close to one hundred individuals (all of them male), of whom one, John Flaxman, was to become a famous sculptor.[328] In 1784, Hindmarsh also had the second edition of *A Treatise concerning Heaven and Hell* printed.

While the Theosophical Society was to dissolve within less than a decade, Hindmarsh did not give up the idea of organising a group of people interested in Swedenborg's work. With himself as leader, a separatist group originating within the Theosophical Society established itself as a church, and asked Robert Hindmarsh's father, the Methodist minister James Hindmarsh, to lead its first service of worship on January 27, 1788. Today, the Swedenborgian 'Church of the New Jerusalem' traces its origin back to this event. Without Robert Hindmarsh's enthusiasm for *A Treatise concerning Heaven and Hell*, this event would never have occurred.

The early readers of *A Treatise concerning Heaven and Hell* foreshadowed, and even shaped, the way later generations would respond to the book. Today it is clear that by 1782, the early readers had already formulated the three main responses adopted in the nineteenth and twentieth centuries. Many would follow John Wesley's sharp critique and dismiss *A Treatise concerning Heaven and Hell* as pure fantasy, delusion, heresy, or, worse, as inspired by 'the spirit of darkness'.[329] At times, Wesley comes close to satirizing Swedenborg's views, but for him and his audience, the subject was too serious to be amenable to satirical comment. This changed in the twentieth century, when Mark Twain (1835–1910) published 'Captain Stormfield's Visit to Heaven' (1907).[330] A second group would see *A Treatise concerning Heaven and Hell* the way Swedenborg's French translator, Antoine Joseph Pernety, understood the book: as an introduction to a new, esoteric worldview that permitted the reception of inspiration from spirits or angels. An impressive number of romantic poets and artists appreciated Swedenborg's book or were in some way or other influenced by it; these include William Blake (1757–1827) and Samuel Taylor Coleridge in England, Friedrich Wilhelm Schelling (1775–1854) in Germany, and Honoré de

---

327 Hindmarsh, *Rise and Progress*, p. 23.
328 Hindmarsh, *Rise and Progress*, p. 23.
329 Wesley, 'Thoughts on the Writings of Baron Swedenborg', p. 422.
330 Mark Twain, 'Captain Stormfield's Visit to Heaven', in: *The Bible according to Mark Twain*. Edited by H.G. Baetzold and R.B. McCullough, Athens, Ga. 1995, pp. 129–188.

Balzac in France.³³¹ A third group, represented by Robert Hindmarsh, would either make *A Treatise concerning Heaven and Hell* part of the sacred writings recognised by a new Christian church and accepted as a strong revelatory and theological statement of life after death, or consider it the beginning of a new religious philosophy.

This third group, generally now referred to as the Swedenborgians, can be credited with translating *De Coelo* into many modern languages. One Swedenborgian, Johann Friedrich Immanuel Tafel (1796–1863), head librarian of the University of Tübingen in Germany, also published a new edition of the original Latin text (1862). Due to the effort of the translators, Emanuel Swedenborg's *De Coelo* ranks as one of the few eighteenth-century religious books still in print and still attracting considerable attention, in comparison to many other writings dating from the same period. Thanks to them, *De Coelo* can still be discovered as a work that has, as Tessin remarked, 'so many new and unexpected turns that it may be read through without boredom'.

---

331 There is substantial evidence for Swedenborg's influence on romanticism; research has focussed on Balzac, Blake, Coleridge, Emerson, Goethe, Novalis, and Schelling. America's most important romantic movement: Transcendentalism, was deeply influenced by Swedenborg. Two embodiments of the French romantic temper: otherworld-utopias and spiritualism, also seem to include a Swedenborgian element, see Thomas A. Kselman, *Death and the Afterlife in Modern France*, Princeton 1993, pp. 143–162.

Appendix

Thomas Hartley on Swedenborg's Doctrine of Correspondences (1778)

Hartley was Swedenborg's first English translator. His English version of *De commercio animae et corporis* was published in 1770, when Swedenborg was still alive. Later he reworked William Cookworthy's translation of *De Coelo* for publication in 1778 as *A Treatise concerning Heaven and Hell*. This book includes a long preface by Hartley. With more than fifty large pages of text, it constitutes the first English defence of, and detailed introduction to, Swedenborg's work. Tafel in his *Documents concerning the Life and Character of Emanuel Swedenborg* reprints some pages of this preface.[332] The following excerpt comes immediately after that included in Tafel's collection.

[p. xl:] I cannot think of concluding this preface without speaking somewhat particularly to a point of doctrine, the knowledge of which is the more necessary to the reader for the right understanding of the author's writings, as in the vast variety of subjects and new discoveries that he presents to us, it has a principal connection with most of them; nay, is the true key in his hand that opens the secrets of the visible and invisible worlds, explains man to himself, and also reveals the spiritual sense of the Sacred Writings. The doctrine I am here speaking of, is that of cor- [p. xli] respondency or correspondences, which are terms nearly of the same signification.

Correspondence or correspondency, in a philosophical sense, is a kind of analogy that one thing bears to another, or the manner in which one thing represents, images, or answers to another; and this doctrine, as it refers to things in heaven and in earth according to their mutual relations, is given us in the following adage of the renowned Hermes Trismegistus – *Omnia quae in coelis, sunt in terris terrestri modo; omnia quae in terris, sunt in coelis coelesti modo* [all that is in heaven, is also on earth, albeit in a terrestrial manner; all that is on earth, is also in heaven, albeit in a celestial way].

This natural or material world, in which we live as to the body, proceeds derivatively (in a sense consistent with the Mosaick account of the creation) from the spiritual world, and subsists by continual influx from it; it is a spiritual thing formed into a palpable and material thing, as an essence clothing itself with a form; or as a soul making to itself a body. Therefore this world, and all things in it, as far forth as they stand in the divine order, do correspond to heaven and heavenly things; but now (through the fall of man) standing in evil as well as good, the dark, evil, or hellish world has gained a form in outward nature. Hence it is, that so many evil men, evil beasts, and poisonous things, together with all the disorders in the natural world, bear its impressions and properties, and make this world a kind of torment-house to us. Man, considered in himself, is a little image of heaven or hell, and also of this outward world, which no other being is; and therefore he is the most wonderful of all God's creatures. At death he puts off his part in this material kingdom, and passes into one of the other two, being its servant to which he obeys or unites himself here by his will and affections; and therefore he is commanded to set his 'affections on things above' (Col. iii.2), as they constitute the band of union betwixt heaven and hell, and the soul of man. These three worlds are called Principles, as first, the light or heavenly world; secondly, the dark or hellish world; and thirdly,

---

332 Thomas Hartley, Preface to Emanuel Swedenborg, *A Treatise concerning Heaven and Hell*, London 1778, pp. xxxi–xxxiii, xxxix–xl = Rudolf Leonard Tafel, *Documents concerning the Life and Character of Emanuel Swedenborg*, London 1890, vol. 2/3, pp. 506–510.

this natural or material world; and man's reasoning faculty stands in the center of the three, and receives [p. xlii:] impressions from each, as it turns to one or other of them; then speculates on the material it derives thence, and contends for or against right and truth, even as the affections are set, for these bias, lead, or bribe it; and therefore, if reason be not enlightened from above, ready to enlist on any side.

The human nature was so almost universally corrupted at the time of our Savior's advent in the flesh, that unless Jesus Christ had come into the world when He did, to restore the heavenly principle of light and grace, or truth and goodness, through the medium of his humanity (all immediate communication between God and the soul being well nigh ceased) the human race must have perished, by falling irrecoverably into the evil principle, to the utter extinction of truth, and the loss of all free will to good; but by the entrance of this Divine Friend into the human nature, He opened the shut gate of communication betwixt heaven and earth, God and the soul, and so became our great Mediator and gracious Redeemer. But still we are at liberty to receive or reject Him as our Sanctification and complete Redemption, for man can only be saved consistently with choice and free will.

Man had lost the true original language of nature (which expressed things according to their qualities and properties) before the flood, even so much of it as had remained among the posterity of Seth and Enoch for a considerable time; and this ignorance they fell into on their losing the knowledge of nature in its correspondence to divine and heavenly things; for nature in its proper order, as observed before, is the book of God, and exhibits spiritual things in material forms. In the room therefore of this was substituted a language by letters and reading in books, to help him this way for attaining to divine knowledge, as rudiments leading thereto in our present state of ignorance, in which literature is mistaken by most for wisdom itself; however, to some the door was and still is open for immediate heavenly communications, but what through unbelief, earthly mindedness, and other sad impediments, few at this time are qualified for so high a privilege.

[p. xliii] The early ancients after the flood had some knowledge of correspondency derived down to them by tradition, though without any perception of it in themselves; and it remained longest among the Egyptians, of which their hieroglyphicks or sacred sculptures were a principal part; but by degrees they became so far corrupted and blind, as to loose sight of the things represented, and to worship their representatives or images. Hence the original of their foolish idolatry of beasts, birds, fishes, and vegetables. Our enlightened author, had he lived longer, designed, as he told me, to give us the key to the ancient hieroglyphical learning, saying, at the same time, that none but himself could do it; but of this the world was not worthy.

The knowledge of correspondences is now almost entirely lost, especially in Europe, where even the name is little understood; and this is one main cause of the obscurity of the Scriptures of the Old Testament, which were chiefly written by the rules of this science; nay, man also, as an image of the spiritual and natural worlds, contains in himself the correspondences of both, of the former in his interior, and of the latter in his exterior or bodily part, and so is called the Microcosm, or Little World. Thus for example; all the organs of his senses, his features, bowels, and vessels, even to the minutest vein and nerve, correspond to something in the soul or spiritual part. On the other hand, the affections and passions of the mind represent themselves naturally in the face and features, so that the countenance would be the natural index to the mind, were men in a state of simplicity, without guile and dissimulation; and yet, as matters stand at present, so much still appears of the mind in the correspondent features of the face, as to serve for a type, signature, or impression thereof. [...] [p. xlv:] It is hoped, that what has been here offered on the subject of correspondency, will be found useful to such as are in a disposition to give the following book an attentive perusal.

Chapter 7: American Heavens. An Exploration of Cemeteries, 1740–1850

> Those who no longer go to church still go to the cemetery.[333]
> Philippe Ariès

While changing attitudes toward death and dying have been extensively studied by recent scholarship, ideas concerning life after death remain a neglected field of research. This essay argues that between 1740 and 1850 a dramatic change occurred in the way many American Christians, especially mainstream Protestants, saw their eternal fate in the afterlife. While the church-centred Puritan view of heaven featured bodily resurrection and an eternity of divine worship, liberal nineteenth-century theologians redefined both the quality and the activities of paradise. They ignored the concept of bodily resurrection and transformed heaven into a place where married partners and families met, never again to part. At the same time, the spacious and scenic rural cemetery replaced the narrow urban churchyard. Since the corpse was no longer seen as the property of God and his earthly representatives, the funeral soon became a family affair with a privately owned grave.

It is particularly in cemeteries that we can see how the new ideas of life after death emerged. Accordingly, the sources considered in this paper include symbols on gravestones, sentimental epitaphs, and the location of cemeteries. Popular literature on life beyond the grave supplements and elucidates such evidence. Thus material and intellectual culture receive equal attention.

Puritan heaven

In early eighteenth-century Puritan New England the funeral was much more than just a family affair.[334] Upon the death of a family member the head of a household would inform relatives, friends, and the local minister. Then they assembled in the house of the deceased before silently processing with the corpse to the cemetery, usually a churchyard or a fenced area close to the meetinghouse.

---

333 Philippe Ariès, *Western Attitudes toward Death*, Baltimore 1974, p. 73.
334 David E. Stannard, *The Puritan Way of Death*, New York 1977; Gordon E. Geddes, *Welcome Joy: Death in Puritan New England*, Ann Arbor, Mich. 1981.

Although there was some pomposity and display of wealth in the giving of gloves and rings to those invited or even all who attended, Puritans kept the actual burial ceremony as simple as possible, avoiding the Catholic ritualism their divines so uncompromisingly disavowed.

At the grave the minister said a prayer and sometimes gave an address that extolled the known, or not-so-known, virtues of the passed member of his flock. More frequently, the funeral oration was delivered at the next regular Thursday or Sunday service. In his address the minister might recall what the catechism of the New England Primer taught about the fate of body and soul after death. 'The souls of believers are at their death made perfect in holiness', wrote the Primer, 'and do immediately pass into glory, and their bodies being still united to Christ, do rest in their graves till the resurrection.'[335] Death involved the separation of body and soul; the former would stay in the grave, while the latter might pass either into heavenly glory or into the torment of hell, whichever was deserved.

Generally the minister would not dare to assert which was applicable, heaven or hell, for a stern Puritan doctrine emphasised human ignorance on such matters. This caution did not prevent the preacher from expatiating on a general resurrection that would reunite bodies and souls, thus making the restored elect 'perfectly blessed in full enjoying of God, to all eternity'[336]. Until this resurrection, which was vaguely thought of as an event in the distant future, the glorified souls 'go on in their white robes to do the parts of priests before him', that is, before God himself. The souls' primary heavenly activity was the continuous worship of God as described in the New Testament. The less fortunate, of course, would have to go to a 'place of torment'. 'In that place', explained Cotton Mather in a funeral sermon of 1717, 'they are with horror expecting the greater torment that will at the Day of Judgment be inflicted upon them.'[337]

If they could afford to do so, the relatives marked the grave with a simple headstone that indicated the name of the dead, the date of death, the age, and occasionally some more information about the life of the interred person. The opening line of the epitaph usually read, 'Here lies the body of …' or, 'Here lie the remains of …'.[338] Sometimes the personal data were followed by a lyrical epitaph addressed to the reader, reminding him or her of the inevitability of death, as well as the Christian duty to be well-prepared. A typical epitaph reads:

---

335 *The New England Primer 1727.* Edited by Paul L. Floyd, New York 1899, no pagination.
336 *The New England Primer 1727.*
337 Ronald E. Bosco (ed.), *The Puritan Sermon in America 1630–1750,* Delmar, N.Y. 1978, vol. 4, p. 110 and p. 116.
338 Michel Vovelle, 'A Century and One-Half of American Epitaphs 1660–1813', *Comparative Studies in Society and History* 22 (1980), pp. 534–547, at p. 541.

Come mortal man
and cast an eye come read thy doom
prepare to die.
(1740, Newburyport, Mass.)[339]

There were of course simpler epitaphs such as 'Reserved for a glorious resurrection' or, 'Gone, but not lost' – two epitaphs Cotton Mather recommended for the gravestones of children who died in infancy.[340] More effusive texts praised the moral and religious qualities of the deceased, but rarely referred to private virtues. One epitaph dating from 1709 which called a pastor not only 'a fruitful Christian', but also 'a tender husband, and a parent kind, a faithful friend' (Wakefield, Mass.)[341] is the exception rather than the rule. On early eighteenth-century gravestones a stern and icy tone prevailed.

The unsentimental attitude of Puritans was reflected in the art with which they almost uniformly decorated their gravestones. While the sides of most stones were embellished with simple floral and geometric motifs, the top of the stone was decorated with a symmetrical, winged skull. Not unlike a printed letterhead, it dominated and determined the message inscribed on the stone. Like the images of bones, hourglasses, coffins, and palls that were sometimes added, the skull is a powerful and realistic symbol of death. It represents the actual dead person, thus reminding the onlooker that putrefaction was a grim, inescapable reality. The wings, on the other hand, symbolise the soul's journey to another world, be it heaven or hell. The motif seems to have been inspired by Psalm 90:10 –

> The days of our years are threescore years and ten;
> and if by reason of strength they be forescore years,
> yet is their strength labor and sorrow;
> for it is soon cut off, and we fly away.

The winged skull is a concise, condensed statement of the Puritan doctrine of death and after-life. It survives as one of the very few symbols permitted to the sculptor who worked in a culture essentially hostile to iconic representation.

The sometimes individually designed headstone, the personal epitaph, and the prominent role of the family in the funeral procedure should not mislead us. Puritan death, and life after death, was not a family matter that belonged to the private realm. A closer look at some of the ideas and practices involved in the funerary complex reveals that Puritan death was an eminently public event.

---

339 Dickran Tashjihan and Ann Tashjihan, *Memorials for Children of Change: The Art of Early New England Stonecarving*, Middleton, Conn. 1974, p. 279.
340 Edmund S. Morgan, *The Puritan Family*, New York 1966, p. 184.
341 David H. Watters, *'With Bodilie Eyes'. Eschatological Themes in Puritan Literature and Gravestone Art*, Ann Arbor, Mich. 1981, p. 110.

Consequently, it had to be dealt with by the community rather than by the bereaved family alone. By giving such mourning paraphernalia as gloves, rings, and scarves, the bereaved family tried to attract a large crowd to the funeral and involve as many people as possible in the ritual. Thus, communal solidarity was symbolically re-enacted and affirmed.

In 1742, New England legislation tried to limit this extravagant and costly gift-giving by transforming it into a payment given to the minister and the bearers of the coffin.[342] Yet, the communal character of the funeral remained. Legislation underscored, if only implicitly, the official role of the minister. Even though Puritan theology held that the minister attended the funeral as a private individual, one participant amongst others, he must still be viewed as a representative of a religious body for whose values he stood and whose ideas he explained in public prayer and address. Only in theory was there a difference between a minister's merely participatory and truly official roles. 'Although centred in the family, the funeral was a communal affair', asserts one historian; 'the community gathered, ate and drank, marched in procession, and met the need of closing its own ranks at the loss of a member.'[343]

The practice of burying the dead in the churchyard or in a burial ground situated on the town commons at the edge of the settlement, provides another important clue to understanding the public nature of Puritan death. The public character of the town commons is evident, and so is the communal quality of the churchyard. Its very location defines the churchyard as an extension of the church itself. Being buried at the place of public worship the dead still belong to the worshipping community of which they mystically form a part. This is the time-honoured Christian idea of the 'communion of saints', the idea that the dead as well as the living members of the church belong together and form one community. The public character of the cemetery is further enhanced by its actual appearance. Cluttered with virtually identical gravestones, indistinguishable except for their inscriptions, it reminds us of the Puritan congregation whose identically dressed members met in their simple church. In the graveyard the dead Christians form a silent, petrified congregation. It replicates the living church members who worship their God in the meetinghouse, and the departed souls standing around the divine throne in heaven. In the cemetery as a public place the bodies silently await one final event that will concern all without discrimination: the general resurrection of the dead.

The corpse, therefore, does not belong to the family of the deceased, but to the community. It is public property. Even more than during life, when a man or

---

342 Geddes, *Welcome Joy*, p. 144.
343 Geddes, *Welcome Joy*, p. 153.

woman could be excluded from the church or resign from membership, he or she is the inalienable property of all. One could also say that the corpse belongs to God and, therefore, to the church as his earthly representative. Both explanations amount to the same thing, saying that the dead are lost to their relatives, but not to the community as a whole.

It is in keeping with this that in the eighteenth century the bier and the pall that covered the coffin during the procession were usually either the property of churches, and under their management, or belonged to the civic community and were in the hands of the civil authorities. More importantly, this was true of New England cemeteries, which were typically owned by the town.[344]

In spite of the fact that many New England burial grounds are adjacent to the sites of old meetinghouses and churches, they were legally unrelated. While the church would receive only its members, the civic graveyard would eventually accommodate everyone – saint and sinner, Christian and atheist, the deceased's coffin being draped with the communal pall. In either case the cemetery and the interred bodies belonged to the realm of the community and the public, rather than that of the family.

The transformation of Puritan heaven

Uncertainty about the soul's ultimate fate, aptly expressed by the winged skull that could fly either to hell or heaven, and the funeral as a public, communal affair, were the hallmark of Puritan dealings with death. Within the six decades following 1740, however, things changed rapidly.[345]

The first ten years of this period are known as the Great Awakening, a religious revival that simultaneously involved most of American Protestantism. By stirring up religious sentiments it brought a re-orientation of religious life and thought. This movement, the best-known representative of which is Jonathan Edwards, propagated a new religious ideal. Pre-revival Puritanism had believed

---

344 Allen I. Ludwig, *Graven Images: New England Stonecarving and its Symbols, 1650–1815*, Middleton, Conn. 1966, p. 54; Geddes, *Welcome Joy*, pp. 133. 145–147.

345 Edwin Dethlefsen and James Deetz, 'Death's Heads, Cherubs and Willow Trees: Experimental Archaeology in Colonial Cemeteries', *American Antiquity* 31 (1965/66), pp. 502–510; idem, 'Death's Head, Cherub, Urn and Willow', *Natural History* 76 (March 1967), pp. 28–37; James Robert Armstrong, *Trends in American Eschatology* (Diss. Boston College), Chesnut Hill, Mass. 1976; Peter Benes, *The Masks of Orthodoxy: Folk Gravestone Carving in Plymouth County, Mass., 1689–1805*, Amherst 1977; Vovelle, 'A Century and One-Half of American Epitaphs'.

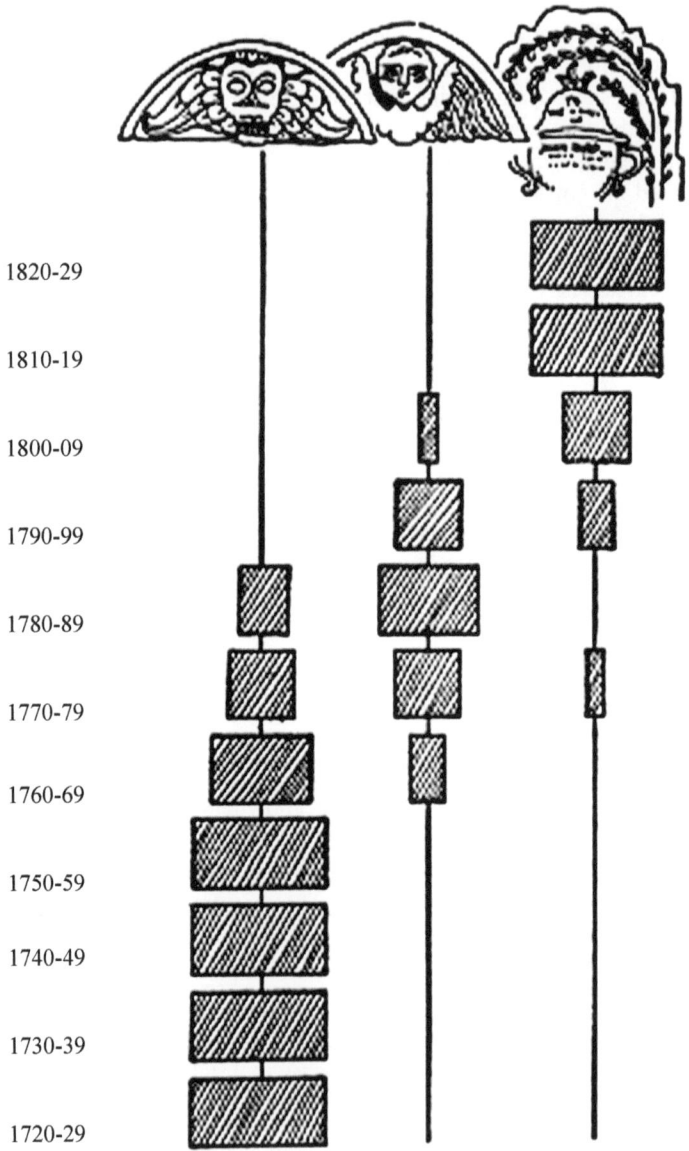

7.1 From winged skull to cherub to inscribed urn. – The development of gravestone design in the cemetery of Stoneham, Massachusetts suggests a movement away from grim notions of death towards more pleasant and personal conceptions.

in predestination. God had either elected the individual as a future member of the heavenly kingdom, or rejected him or her, thus providing hell with another denizen. Since only God could save a soul from the torments of hell, as well as from temporal misfortunes, passive obedience to God's commandments was the only option. Instead of such compliance, the revivalists preached repentance, humiliation, and the creation of a burning faith in the redemptive power of Christ. These conditions were within the control of 'sinners' rather than God. Grace no longer was restricted to those already 'elected'. Salvation, therefore, was more tangible and closer at hand than ever before. Popular expectations of salvation – going to heaven after death – increased considerably.

This new trend manifested itself visibly in the design of gravestones. While the overall structure – a rectangular plate for ornaments and text – remained identical, the design at the top changed between 1760 and 1780 (see Figs. 7.1 and 7.2).

7.2 Winged skull and cherub. – These decorations typical of eighteenth-century gravestones symbolise the soul of the deceased human person. The skull emphasises the grim aspect of death, while the cherub seems to anticipate the soul's heavenly ascent.

The winged skull was replaced by a winged human head, now generally termed a 'cherub' or an 'angel'. Just like the winged skull it refers to the soul's migration to the other world. While the skull-soul may go either to heaven or hell, the cherub betrays the new assurance of salvation; God's world rather than the devil's would be its ultimate destination. The soul would join the angelic choirs.

The same trend can be discerned in the epitaphs whose references to the body and bodily resurrection become a rare feature. Beginning in 1780, the image of direct transition to the other world notably prevails over that of a delay. At the same time allusions to the final judgment and resurrection become less frequent and more discreet. People came to believe in 'instant salvation' after death rather than in the complex and seemingly contradictory dogma of an instant personal and a distant universal judgment. Now people died in the hope, and indeed in anticipation of, the joy and glory that was their due by virtue of both their merits and the blood of Christ. The ruler of the paradise to which they gained access was described more often as Redeemer than as Almighty King (with three times more references to saviour than to almighty, according to Michel Vovelle). The new heaven flooded with divine light was the abode of angels whose presence and whose choirs were equally cited. Taking their seat among angels implied that the deceased themselves became angels. Dwelling with the just, the saints, and sometimes with the patriarchs, angels populated that 'happy mansion' where God had prepared a place for the blessed eternity of the newcomer.

The new sense that the soul has taken its definitive and eternal place in heaven is also visible in the epitaph's opening phrase (Table 7.3).

While the old Puritan gravestone marked the burial place of *the body* or *the remains* of the deceased ('here lies the body of ...'), its late eighteenth-century successor was a *monument* ('this monument is erected to the memory of ...'). The tomb was first viewed as a place where the body was placed to await resurrection. Later this idea was no longer pressed with the same force. The tombstone stood for the memory of the deceased whose soul had passed into the other world. Without necessarily having this precise implication, the new key formula helped to bypass the traditional doctrine of bodily resurrection. It was politely ignored or simply forgotten.

Another feature as important and striking as the 'instant heaven' is the new emphasis on the nuclear family as an emotional, if not sentimental, unit. Eighteenth-century epitaphs increasingly stress the domestic virtues of the deceased. It was the tender father, the affectionate, irreplaceable, and unforgettable wife and mother who were mourned.

	17th cent.	1700–40	1740–60	1760–80	1780–00	1800–13
1. 'here lies the body / lie the remains'	100	90	80	43	17	19%
2. 'monument to the memory of'	–	10	18	53	82	80%
3. professional life	56	29	12	25	7	14%
4. misfortunes	–	–	5	16	16	23%
5. religious qualities	30	80	52	57	34	49%
6. family qualities	18	28	30	29	22	37%
7. expression of regrets	12	4	15	11	28	31%
8. assertion of familial group	6	–	–	11	17	20%

Table 7.3: Major themes in American epitaphs. The expression of family values and sentiments increases, and culminates in the nineteenth century.

Toward the end of the eighteenth century, the right to shed tears is recognised. Lamentation is not hidden, but engraved in stone, and often the misfortunes of the deceased, shared by the family, are tearfully chronicled. When one member of the family suffers from illness or bad luck, the whole group is emotionally involved. The family group, at times enlarged to include friends or fellow citizens, made its entry into the epitaph. It affirmed the recognition of or the affection felt by those who erected and dedicated the monument. With the emergence and appreciation of the deceased as a 'private man', the 'public man', whose professional career many Puritan epitaphs had dutifully chronicled, faded away.

The birth of Victorian heaven

Around 1800, New Englanders abandoned the cherub design of headstones and replaced it with the urn-and-willow motif, which became characteristic of Victorian cemeteries.[346]

The new decoration was adopted as a fitting expression of the grief, mourning, and regret families experienced at the death of one of their members. The urn suggested the idea of a Greek-style monument, while the weeping willow with its hanging boughs is a conventional emblem of mourning. (The urn was not a container of cremation ashes. Cremation was introduced only in late nineteenth-century America.) Like contemporaneous architecture and fashion modelled on Greco-Roman prototypes, it foreshadows the conspicuous display of mourning in the Victorian celebration of death, as well as the wish to give the tomb a picturesque setting in an elegant, well-kept park. A mournful symbol of sentiment has taken the place of an image of hope.

This is not to say, however, that the hope of an afterlife had declined or even vanished. The hope, and indeed the certainty, of heavenly bliss were openly and frequently expressed in lyrical epitaphs. As heaven had already become a place to which one would ascend immediately, it easily could be assimilated to this world, and made to conform to its predominately domestic values. A place as close as heaven could not be essentially different from earth, or more precisely from home. Heaven, the transcendent home, must be a place where one would find and rejoin one's beloved. This new idea emerged shortly before 1800, and soon gained currency as expressed by grieving spouses and despairing parents. The innovation can be found on several gravestones of 1797.[347] The rector of the Swedish churches in Pennsylvania, for instance, dedicated an inscription to his deceased wife. 'He erected', it says, 'this monumental record of her piety,

---

346 Dethlefsen and Deetz, 'Death's Heads, Cherubs, and Willow Trees'; idem, 'Death's Head, Cherub, Urn and Willow'; Blanche M.G. Linden, 'The Willow Tree and Urn Motif: Changing Ideas about Death and Nature', in: *Markers*, Worcester, Mass. 1979/80, vol. 1, pp. 149–155.
347 Timothy Alden, *A Collection of American Epitaphs and Inscriptions*, 5 vols., New York 1814, nos. 104, 671, and 974.
I cannot verify the date 'around 1760' suggested by Vovelle, 'A Century and One-Half of American Epitaphs', p. 544. There must be similar epitaphs dating from before 1797. One example, unfortunately undated (later than 1739), is from the Warner Hall Farm near Naxera, Va.: 'Here sleeps the body of Isabella Clayton, while her soul is gone in triumph to meet the best of husbands and never more to be divorced by him' (*Epitaphs of Gloucester and Mathews Counties in Tidewater Virginia through 1865*, Richmond, Va. 1959, p. 96). Numerous nineteenth-century examples can be found in William B. Moore and Stephen C. Davis, 'Rosa is an Angel Now: Epitaphs from Crawford County, Pennsylvania', *The Western Pennsylvania Historical Magazine* 58 (1975), pp. 1–51, 185–253, 327–394.

kindness, economy, neatness; her faithful affection to him in many trying scenes; of his grief, which shall not cease *until they meet in the land of the living*' (1797, Philadelphia).[348]

Another stone, dedicated to a widow who died soon after her husband, celebrates her day of passing as the time when 'she commenced her inseparable union with her much beloved consort' (1800, Plymouth, Mass.).[349]

To the readers of Emanuel Swedenborg's *Delights of Wisdom concerning Conjugal Love* (Philadelphia 1796) and *A Treatise concerning Heaven and Hell* (Baltimore 1812) these ideas sounded thoroughly familiar. The *Christian Examiner* of 1824 refers to the expectation of meeting friends in the other world as a matter of fact ('On the Future Life', 1824). Starting in 1833 America's bookstores were flooded with popular and semi-popular books on the social aspects and joys of life after death.[350] Typical titles were Richard Mant, *The Happiness of the Blessed* (Philadelphia 1833), Benjamin Dorr, *The Recognition of Friends in Another World* (Philadelphia 1838), and Henry Harbaugh, *The Heavenly Home* (Philadelphia 1853). In the forty years between 1833 and 1873, more than forty such titles were published, and many of them went through numerous editions. The authors were Reformed or Evangelical clergymen, Episcopalians, Unitarians, Moravians, Swedenborgians, and Spiritualists. A Catholic version was *In Heaven We Know Our Own* (New York 1863), originally written in French by the Jesuit François-Rene Blot.

There are differences among these authors. Unitarians do not distinguish between God and Jesus as the focus of heavenly existence, and they believe in eternal spiritual activity and progress rather than rest. Catholics have their purgatory as a place where the soul is prepared for its eventual admission to paradise. Swedenborgians repeat, with great rhetorical skill, their master's assertion that married life in heaven will include carnal joys.

Despite such peculiarities, nineteenth-century popular literature on heaven conveys the impression of a vague yet perceptible consensus. There was more assurance of salvation than among the Puritans whose strict doctrine did not

---

348 Alden, *A Collection of American Epitaphs*, no. 974.
349 Alden, *A Collection of American Epitaphs*, no. 618.
350 The authors include Richard Mant (bishop of the Church of England), Henry Harbaugh (German Reformed pastor), Augustus Charles Thompson (Moravian), George Cheever (Congregationalist), Edmund Hamilton Sears (Unitarian), William Henry Holcombe and Benjamin F. Barrett (Swedenborgians), Robert Dale Owen (Spiritualist), and many other, chiefly Protestant writers. For an evaluation of their books see Ann Douglas, 'Heaven Our Home: Consolation Literature in the Northern United States 1830–1880', in: David E. Stannard (ed.), *Death in America*, Philadelphia 1975, pp. 49–68; Marie Caskey, *Chariot of Fire: Religion and the Beecher Family*, New Haven 1978, pp. 294–302.

allow for any knowledge about our election or reprobation, i.e. our going to heaven or hell. Most Christians agreed that after death the soul goes immediately to heaven in order to be rewarded by God and enjoy eternal bliss. There was a corresponding decline of belief in hell.[351] The doctrine of eventual resurrection of the body and its reunion with the soul became less important. Hell and resurrection were often ignored. Both theological and popular authors emphasised the social enjoyments of heaven as well as its domestic nature: friends and relatives would be reunited, mothers would find their lost children, wives their husbands, etc. Some of the more daring authors, including the Anglican bishop Richard Mant and the French Jesuit Blot, suggested that the marriage bond would continue beyond the grave.

One also gets the impression that the divine centre of traditional Puritan heaven became modified if not less important. In his Easter sermon of 1834, noted Unitarian William Channing told his Boston congregation that in heaven, Jesus would joyfully welcome any newcomer not from 'a real and elevated throne', but like the humble carpenter and preacher he was on earth.[352] Jesus is just one of the numerous friends Christians want to and indeed will meet in the other life. In the final analysis, people were less interested in meeting God or Jesus than in being reunited with their lost parents, children or spouses. 'As you know to me Heaven is where Father and Mother and Aunt Esther are', mused James Beecher in a letter, 'rather than or I should say, more than where God is. For God is here, they are not' (before 1874).[353] Heaven has become thoroughly anthropocentric – man-centred rather than God-centred – and thus as un-Puritan as is conceivable.

Another, even more striking un-Puritan idea is that of marriage in heaven. In Cotton Mather's view this would be impossible, because 'there will be no different sexes in the Holy City. [...] They will so put on Christ that there will be neither male nor female, nor any more difference between them'. Heavenly man is modelled on Adam as he was before the creation of Eve, that is, he is an asexual male. Women will be translated into this form so that 'the name woman is to be heard no more' (Mather).[354]

Consequently, a heavenly marriage relationship does not make sense in a Puritan context. The Puritan view even discourages consideration of any other

---

351 James I. Farrell, *Inventing the American Way of Death, 1830–1920*, Philadelphia 1980, pp. 82–85.
352 William E. Channing, 'The Future Life: Discourse Preached on Easter Sunday 1834', in: *The Works of William E. Channing*, Boston 1880, p. 361.
353 Caskey, *Chariot of Fire: Religion and the Beecher Family*, pp. 290–291.
354 Quoted in Watters, *'With Bodilie Eyes'. Eschatological Themes in Puritan Literature and Gravestone Art*, pp. 115–116.

form of human relationship in the next world. Samuel Willard's 1726 explanation of the catechism refers only to the negative side of heavenly society. 'The saints shall lay aside all their jealousies and animosities, and with one heart love one another entirely, and join with the most entire unity in the Heavenly Consort (i.e. Christ).' In other words: he excludes the possessiveness that might arise in the individual's love of the deity. The saint will enjoy Christ's 'tender embraces' that were experienced by some mystics even here, 'when Christ took them into his chambers, and spread over them his banner of love; when his left hand was under their head, and his right arm embraced them'.[355] Such intimacy is a possible source of discord and jealousy among the saints and leaves no room for true social relationships among them.

The new attitudes toward mourning and life after death also affected the layout of cemeteries. In the nineteenth-century, the rapid growth of the population necessitated the establishment of new and considerably bigger burial grounds.[356] Between 1790 and 1830, for instance, Boston's population grew from 18.000 to some 61.000 inhabitants. The churchyards and the urban burial ground of the eighteenth-century were overcrowded and seemed not only too small and unsightly, but also offended the growing sense of hygiene. People felt that they were a menace to public health.

The solution suggested by Senator James Hillhouse of New Haven, Connecticut, was to create a private cemetery sponsored by well-to-do citizens. Although New Haven's six-acre New Burial Ground established in 1796 attracted much attention and was highly praised,[357] one generation had to elapse before it was imitated. Boston, Massachusetts, was the first city to follow the example of New Haven. Some citizens of Boston acquired a large parcel of suburban land for a cemetery. The seventy-two acres that were subsequently doubled were situated four miles west of Boston in an area that belonged to Cambridge, seat of the famous Harvard University. From the gentle, wooded slopes of the new 'rural' cemetery one could catch a glimpse both of the college and the city. One could also overlook a fine sweep of the Charles River. Several ponds, as well as numerous shrubs and imposing trees, contributed to the romantic beauty of the spot. The idea was to cultivate a beautiful arboreal garden

---

355 Samuel Willard, *A Compleat Body of Divinity*, Boston 1726, pp. 533–534.
356 Farrell, *Inventing the American Way of Death*, pp. 99–113; Thomas Bender, 'The "Rural" Cemetery Movement: Urban Travail and the Appeal of Nature', *The New England Quarterly* 47 (1974), pp. 196–211; Ann Douglas, *The Feminization of American Culture*, New York 1977, pp. 211–213.
357 Stanley French, 'The Cemetery as Cultural Institution: The Establishment of Mount Auburn and the "Rural Cemetery" Movement', in: Stannard (ed.), *Death in America*, pp. 69–91, at pp. 75–76.

or park into which a cemetery could be integrated in a way that would not damage, but perhaps even enhance its natural beauty. Boston's Mount Auburn cemetery was opened in 1831 and soon became the model of a 'rural cemetery' that every decent American town or city should have. In 1836, Philadelphia established its Laurel Hill cemetery, and Brooklyn's Greenwood followed in 1838. By 1861 there were at least sixty-six garden cemeteries in the United States, all of them modelled on the example of Mount Auburn.

Rural cemeteries imply a significant modification of the eighteenth-century idea and practise of burial. While the Puritan grave belonged to the community, and was typically located near the meetinghouse in town, the Victorian American's grave was owned by the family. Dead bodies, too, were owned by families and were legally treated as the property of the surviving spouse and the next of kin.[358] The grave was situated in a suburban area considered ideal for living. Just like the ideal home, the ideal grave should be beyond the busy, noisy, and often industrial city. In the wake of industrialisation, Americans began not only to romanticise the natural environment, but also claimed it as the proper location of homes for the living as well as the dead.[359]

Rural cemeteries did not belong to churches or towns, but were owned and operated by non-denominational, private companies. These sold individual lots

---

358 Thus the Supreme Court of the State of New York in 1856, approving a report written by Samuel B. Ruggles. This lawyer had argued that the next of kin rather than ecclesiastical authorities hold property rights over a corpse: Samuel B. Ruggles, 'The Law of Burial', in: Alexander W. Bradford, *Reports of Cases Argued and Determind in the Surrogate's Court of the County of New York*, Albany, N.Y. 1857, vol. 4, pp. 503–532. The author of a textbook on *The Law of Cadavers* repeats the argument, summarising the earlier view as follows: 'The church took the body to itself. It held that a corpse was appropriated by it, by divine service and consecrated burial. The spirit departed to the realms of the supernatural; the body was held by the divine agent to await resurrection.' Perceval E. Jackson, *The Law of Cadavers and of Burial and Burial Places*, New York 1936, p. 116. – In continental Europe, legal scholars also consider the dead human body the property of the deceased person's heirs; see Karl Günther Joël, *Die Rechtsverhältnisse am toten Körper*, Quackenbrück 1930 (thesis submitted to the University of Göttingen, Germany).

359 The study of nineteenth-century names is revealing. On the basis of the high frequency of such names as Evergreen, Oak Grove, and Lake View, Zelinsky concludes that 'the nineteenth-century cemetery was emphatically bosky, with the terms *woods, grove, evergreen, forest*, and *sylvan* accounting for 86 per cent of the references to general plant coverage' (p. 183). Like nineteenth-century novelists and their readers he identifies such a landscape with that of heaven which is thought of as 'a monochromatic, evergreen, featuristic land of perpetual spring morning or evening lying under a cloudless, windless, sunny sky, but where brooks and fountains flow nonetheless, and trees, flowering shrubs, and grassy lawns thrive in a park-like ensemble' (p. 191). Wilbur Zelinsky, 'Unearthly Delights: Cemetery Names and the Map of the Changing American Afterworld', in: David Lowenthal et al. (eds.), *Geographies of the Mind*, New York 1976, pp. 171–195.

of about 300 square feet that were neatly marked off as private property, often by fences. Within their lots, people would build subterranean vaults, a stylish house-vault above the ground, a little mausoleum, or just inter their relatives in individual graves. The character of the cemetery as an assemblage of individually or family-owned memorial sites was enhanced by the variety of decorative art, the extent of which was unknown before. 'In the office at the cemetery will be found a large selection of photographs of burial monuments in the modern cemeteries of Italy, recently collected', say the *Regulations* of Philadelphia's West Laurel Hill Cemetery; 'from which new designs can be selected. It is very desirable to avoid, as far as possible, duplicating styles of monuments already in the grounds'.[360] A visit to the still-existing rural cemeteries conveys an impressive contrast with the older churchyards: Puritan uniformity and simplicity had given way to varied and elaborate, if not excessively luxuriant monuments. The place conducive to Puritan meditation on the vanity of life was exchanged for a place of Victorian pomposity and the display of monumental vanities. It is not surprising, then, that rural cemeteries became open-air museums that attracted numerous visitors.

The private character of the cemetery, however, was secured and protected by the bylaws: 'Sundays. Admittance can be granted on this day of the week to funerals, and to the relations and friends accompanying them; or to lotholders on foot with their tickets, (which are in no case transferable) with members of their families, or friends in company.'[361]

Like the burial ground, the corpse itself had moved from communal into family ownership. Consequently, the cemetery should be a place 'where the smitten heart might pour out grief over the grave of the cherished one, secure from the idle gaze of heartless passengers.'[362]

Even inside the cemetery itself people with 'a cultivated and refined taste' preferred a secluded spot for their burials to one that was overlooked. 'Seclusion', explained one cemetery guide, 'is more in unison with the feelings of many friends of the dead than publicity, glare, and notoriety.'[363] It should be clear, however, that the new privacy of the grave and of mourning is not just a random matter of refined taste; it reveals a whole new set of ideas.

---

360 *West Laurel Hill Cemetery/Philadelphia. Description and Regulations.* Edited by the Office of the West Laurel Hill Cemetery Company, 11th ed., Philadelphia 1887, p. 17.
361 *Guide to Laurel Hill Cemetery Near Philadelphia*, Philadelphia 1851, pp. 43–44.
362 *Guide to Laurel Hill Cemetery*, pp. 15–16.
363 Adolphus Strauch, *Spring Grove Cemetery*, Cincinnati 1869, p. 9.

Puritan and Victorian ideas compared

The principle themes we have considered – cemeteries, gravestones, epitaphs, and doctrines of life after death – can now conveniently recapitulated as in the table below (Table 7.4).

	Puritan Heaven – church-oriented (early 18th century)	Victorian Heaven – family-oriented (19th century)
cemetery	churchyard: communal place of ecclesiastical worship; corpse belongs to God and community	rural cemetery: private place of family worship: corpse belongs to family, as does the plot in the cemetery
gravestone	all gravestones uniform, decorated with winged skull ('death's head') as symbol of religious belief	monuments diverse, decorated with urn and willow tree as symbols of mourning
epitaph	short, 'prepare to die' message	long, verbose; the surviving members of the family expect to meet the deceased in the other world
doctrine	uncertainty as to whether the bodiless soul flies to heaven or hell; heaven is God-centred place of eternal worship; saints are asexual	certainty about transition to heaven which is understood as a place where spouses, families, friends reunite; marriage continues

Table 7.4: *Puritan and Victorian notions of heaven. For Puritan Christians, eternal life is God-centred; Victorian heaven has its focus in the family.*

It is not easy to reconstruct the feelings with which a Puritan entered a graveyard. The winged skulls as well as the 'prepare to die' epitaphs no doubt reminded him or her of the uncertainty of salvation, and inspired the fear of eternal damnation in hell. The rural burial grounds of the nineteenth-century, on the other hand, were much more sentimental places, designed for private mourning, unassailed by doubt, in natural surroundings. To the Puritans, nature had meant wilderness, wasteland, a hostile and evil environment, and was even seen as a place of lawlessness and sin.[364] By the end of the eighteenth century, nature had become something not to be feared, but to be admired, capable of elevating the soul, and a source of consolation. Consequently, the rural cemeteries were viewed 'as first schools in the preparation of the heart for a higher culture, as nurseries for an everlasting home', as one author in *The Christian Examiner* explained.[365] The lofty thoughts to be inspired by 'a well-ordered and beautiful cemetery, like our Mount Auburn' were completely individual, personal, and private; the quiet loneliness of the grave would 'strengthen those anticipations which look to a recognition and reunion with departed friends in a future state of existence'.[366]

The private grave situated in a private cemetery was the place where heaven and earth meet. A private piece of land rather than the community of saints was the mystical door to a heaven full of friends, relatives, and spouses.[367]

Postscript

This essay was originally written as a pilot study to explore the heavenly beliefs in early-modern Christianity. The result, but not the essay became part of *Heaven: A History* (1988). The pilot study helped acquire a sense of the chronology of what Colleen McDannell (my co-author) and I came to call the shift from 'theocentric' to 'anthropocentric' notions of life after death. The study of epitaphs permits the historian to see when and how 'anthropocentric' notions became popular – around 1800, as we discovered. Similar studies could be undertaken in European countries, though it is often difficult to find epitaph collections suitable for historical analysis. For France, one may use: Emile Raunié and others, *Epitaphier du vieux Paris. Recueil général des inscriptions funéraires des églises, couvents, collèges, hospices, cimetières et charniers*

---

364 Peter N. Carroll, *Puritanism and the Wilderness*, New York 1969; Linden, 'The Willow Tree and Urn Motif'.
365 J.B., 'Burial of the Dead', *The Christian Examiner* 31 (1842), pp. 137–164, 281–307, at p. 151.
366 J.B., 'Burial of the Dead', pp. 153, 150.
367 The truly public cemeteries are now the national ones, established after 1862 by the United States Government for honourable veterans and soldiers who died in active service. By implication, the bodies of dead soldiers belong to the United States, as does the burial ground which is federal property. The headstones used are of uniform design and size: 13 inches wide, 4 inches thick, and 42 inches high of which 24 are above ground. The inscription always indicates the military rank of the deceased as well as his branch of service. National cemeteries present 'endless vistas of marble headstones, stretching out in unbroken lines like the silent army of the dead standing in review before the succeeding generation of the living' (Karl Decker and Angus McSween, *Historic Arlington*, Washington D.C. 1898, p. 86).

depuis le moyen-âge jusqu'à la fin du XVIIIe siècle, Paris 1890ff., many volumes.

Index

Addison, Joseph 40
afterlife beliefs today 76–77
Almond, Philip 18 n. 15, 34, 113–114
Ambrose of Milan 24–25
America
   heaven in A. 77, 143–159
   See also Edwards, Jonathan
angels
   in Blake 56–57 (with fig. 3.2)
   have a body 113 n. 50
   in Bunyan 47
   in Origen 16
   in Swedenborg 85–87, 103, 135
anthropocentric notions of heaven 11–12, 39, 44, 52–53, 154
   in the Qur'an 41, 64, 126
Ariès, Philippe 143
Asín Palacios, Miguel 65
Assheton, William 36
Augustine 24, 102, 106

Balzac. Honoré de 132, 138–139
baroque culture 109–115
Baxter, Richard 43, 53, 112, 137–138
Bellarmine, Robert 17–18
Bible 29–30, 45, 104
biblical references
   Deut 33,9: 22 n. 32
   Gen 1: 104
   Gen 8,22: 94
   Gen 25,8: 21
   1 John 3,2: 41, 47
   Luke 18,29–30: 45
   Matt 8,12: 88

Ps 11,7: 50 n. 113
Ps 16,3–4: 22 n. 32
Ps 49,15: 22
Rev 5,8: 46
Rev 22,4: 50 n. 113
Blake, William 31, 54–58, 138
   See *also* "The Meeting of a Family in Heaven"
Blot, François-René 74, 153
Bonde, Count Gustaf 123–124
Bonhoeffer, Dietrich 28–29
Boswell, James 27, 41, 111–113
Bultmann, Rudolf 97–98
Bunyan, John *see The Pilgrim's Progress*

cemetery 61, 143–160
Channing, William 154
children in heaven 38, 39, 41, 87
Church of the New Jerusalem 138
Cicero 40
De Coelo & ejus Mirabilibus (Swedenborg) 37–38, 79–142
   translations 128–132
Coleridge, Samuel Taylor 79, 81, 138
corpse, who owns it 156 (with n. 358)
Cuno, Johann Christian 123, 126–127
Cyprian 22, 24

damnation, eternal, *see* punishment, eternal
dead body, *see* corpse
Denis the Carthusian 17
detail, wish for 109–112
Diderot, Denis 93–94
Digby, Kenelm 34

eclecticism 92–94
Edwards, Jonathan 19–21, 37
Emerson, Ralph Waldo 94
England
   heaven in E. 15, 26–28, 34–36, 38–41, 43–59, 77, 112–113
   See also Wesley, John; Almond, Philip

epitaphs
   on American gravestones 144–145, 150–153, 158
   in France 159
   in Spain 61
Erasmus of Rotterdam 107
Escrivá de Balaguer, José Maria 63

Freud, Sigmund 49

Gearing, William 18
The Gentleman's Magazine 27, 40–41, 121, 123, 126 n. 269, 127
God, *see* theocentric notions of heaven
Goethe, Johann Wolfgang 38, 39–40, 43, 109, 115–116 (with n. 255), 121

Hartley, Thomas 128–130, 140–142
heaven in early-modern thought 33–41, 109–115
Heaven: A History (McDannell & Lang) 11–12, 15, 17–18, 22, 25, 28, 159
Heaven and Hell (Swedenborg), see *De Coelo & ejus Mirabilibus*
hell, *see* punishment, eternal; Swedenborg, Emanuel
Hindmarsh, Robert 121, 131, 137–138
Hume, David 111

Jesus 29–30, 107
John of the Cross 67, 68
Johnson, Samuel 27, 41, 112–113

Kant, Immanuel 35, 38 n. 85, 115
kinetic revolution 15–21
Kircher, Athanasius 112
Klopstock, Friedrich 92

Last Judgment 44–45, 96–98
Lavater, Johann Caspar 38, 115–116, 121
Leibniz, Gottfried Wilhelm 19, 35, 94, 102, 106, 113
Lenz, Johann Christoph 128
Less, Gottfried 19
Levites 22
Luis de León 67, 69–71

marriage in heaven 38, 45, 50, 58, 87, 119, 153, 154
Martin of Cochem 36
Martyrdom of Perpetua and Felicity 23–24
Mather, Increase 19
McDannell, Colleen 11, 15
"The Meeting of a Family in Heaven" (Blake) 31, 54–59 (with fig. 3.1), 59
Milton, John 40–41, 43–44, 134
Moltmann, Jürgen 21
Montanism 24
More, Henry 34–35, 102, 113–114
movement in heaven 36
   See also kinetic revolution
Muhammad's journey to heaven 64–65
music and singing in heaven 44, 47
mysticism, Spanish 67–71

Neoplatonism 98–103
Nicholas of Cusa 108
Nicole, Pierre 118–119
Novalis 119

Origen 14–15, 102
Osservatore Romano 28 n. 57

Pernety, Antoine Joseph 131–132
Perpetua *see Martyrdom of Perpetua and Felicity*
The Pilgrim's Progress (Bunyan) 27, 38–39, 43–59
   anthropocentric heaven in *P.P.* 52–53
   theocentric heaven in *P.P.* 46–47, 50–51
Plato 93, 98
Plotinus 98–103
popular culture 5, 25 n. 45, 71–74
Porphyry 103
punishment, eternal in hell
   in Bunyan 48
   self-inflicted by the damned 34, 35, 37
   in Swedenborg 81–83 (will fig. 5.1), 87–90, 136
Puritanism 19, 43, 143–151

Qur'an 41, 64, 126

Rahner, Karl 29–30
Raimundus Lullus 65–66
Renaissance 25, 69, 103–109
reunion, heavenly
   in early Christianity 22–25
   in early-modern times 25–27, 153
   in *The Pilgrim's Progress* (Bunyan) 47–54
   in the twentieth century 28–30, 61,
   in popular culture 5, 25 n. 45
   believed in by P. Benedict XVI 28 n. 57
Richardson, Jonathan 111
Rinser, Luise 29–30
Romanticism 115–119
Rousseau, Jean-Jacques 39, 88

Sheol 22
singing and music in heaven 44, 49
Spain
   heaven in S. 18, 61–77
The Spectator 40
Suárez, Francisco 18
Swedberg, Jesper 37, 86
Swedenborg, Immanuel 37–38, 44, 58, 75, 79–121, 153
   chronology 121
   correspondences, doctrine of 140–142
   on God 37, 90–92, 135
   on heaven 81–83 (with fig. 5.1), 86–87
   on hell 81–83 (will fig. 5.1), 87–90, 136
   on marriage in heaven 45, 87, 153
   reactions to S. 123–142
Switzerland
   heaven in S. *see* Lavater; Rousseau

Teresa of Avila 67, 69, 74, 132
Tessin, Carl Gustaf 121, 123, 124–126, 139
theocentric notions of heaven 11–12, 39, 44, 46–47, 49–51, 53, 63, 144
   in Islam 65
   See also Nicole, Pierre
Thomas Aquinas 18
Troeltsch, Ernst 28

Unamuno, Miguel de 75–76

Valla, Lorenzo 105
Voltaire 111

Watts, Isaac 36–37
Wesley, John 121, 133–137
Whitelocke, Bulstrode 26
worldview, archaic 94–98

Zwingli, Ulrich 107